Tips for Using This Book

I0489183

1. We have printed the pictures on one side of the page only to avoid pencil impression on next page and to protect each individual picture. A sheet of loose rough paper under the page you are working on will offer additional protection to the pages underneath.

2. Start with any page that grabs your interest- who says you need to start from the beginning?

3. Be FREE and color how you desire. There is no thumb rule. There is no "WRONG" way.

4. For the Stress-Relieving coloring experience, Reduce noise and other distractions while coloring. Coloring with Focus and Intention is calming and nurturing for your spirit

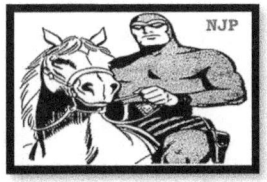

Digital Comics World
By: Satyanveshi
Copyright © 2016

Introduction

Here are Coloring made with original illustrations from Comic books (Marvel, DC Comics) & illustrated versions famous Books.

You will also find original drawings to print created by users and inspired by classics of the so-called "popular" literature: The Lord of the Rings, Harry Potter etc.

At your pens, brushes or pencils, to give life to all these mythical characters, thanks to the colors you choose!

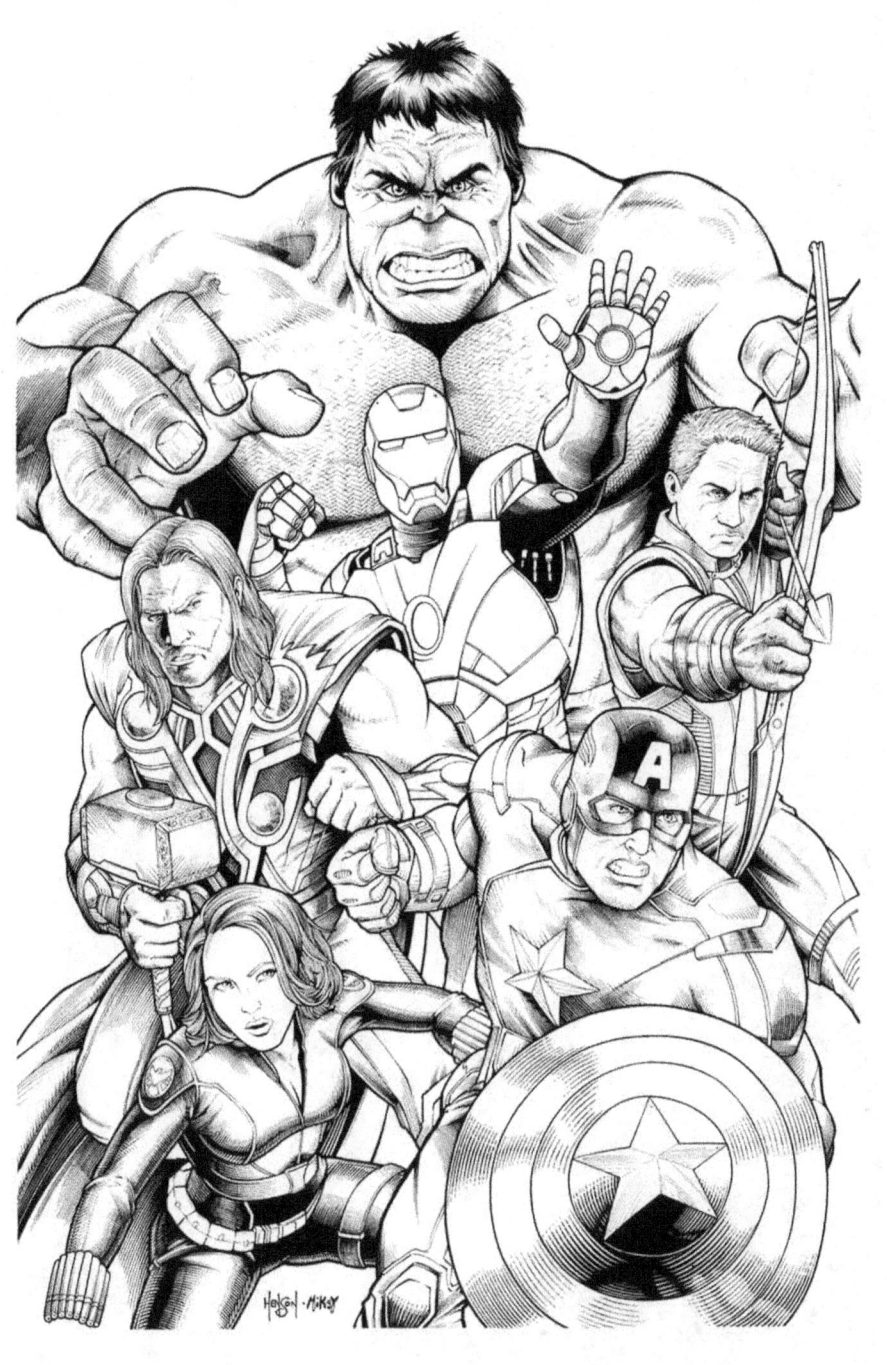

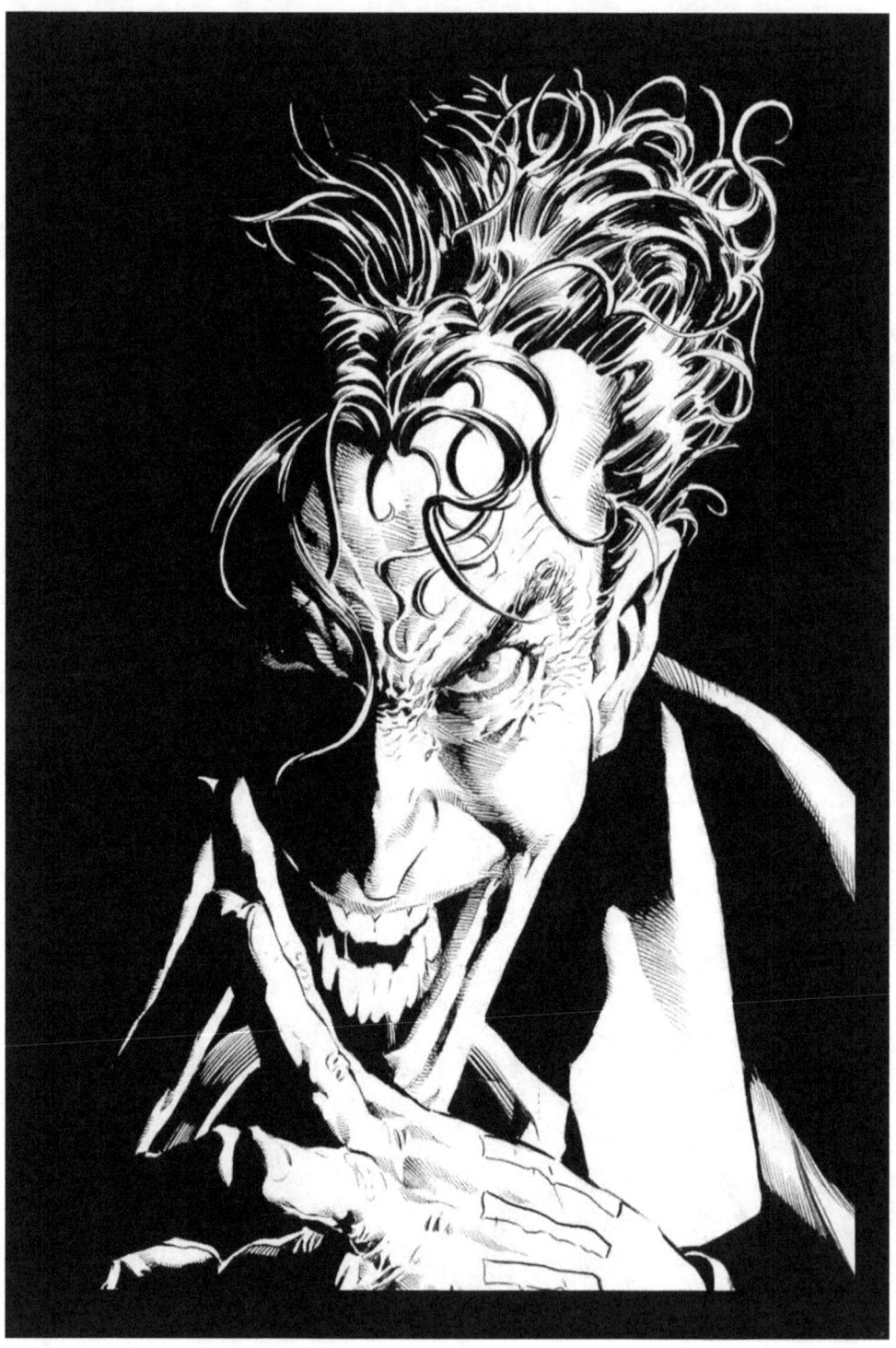

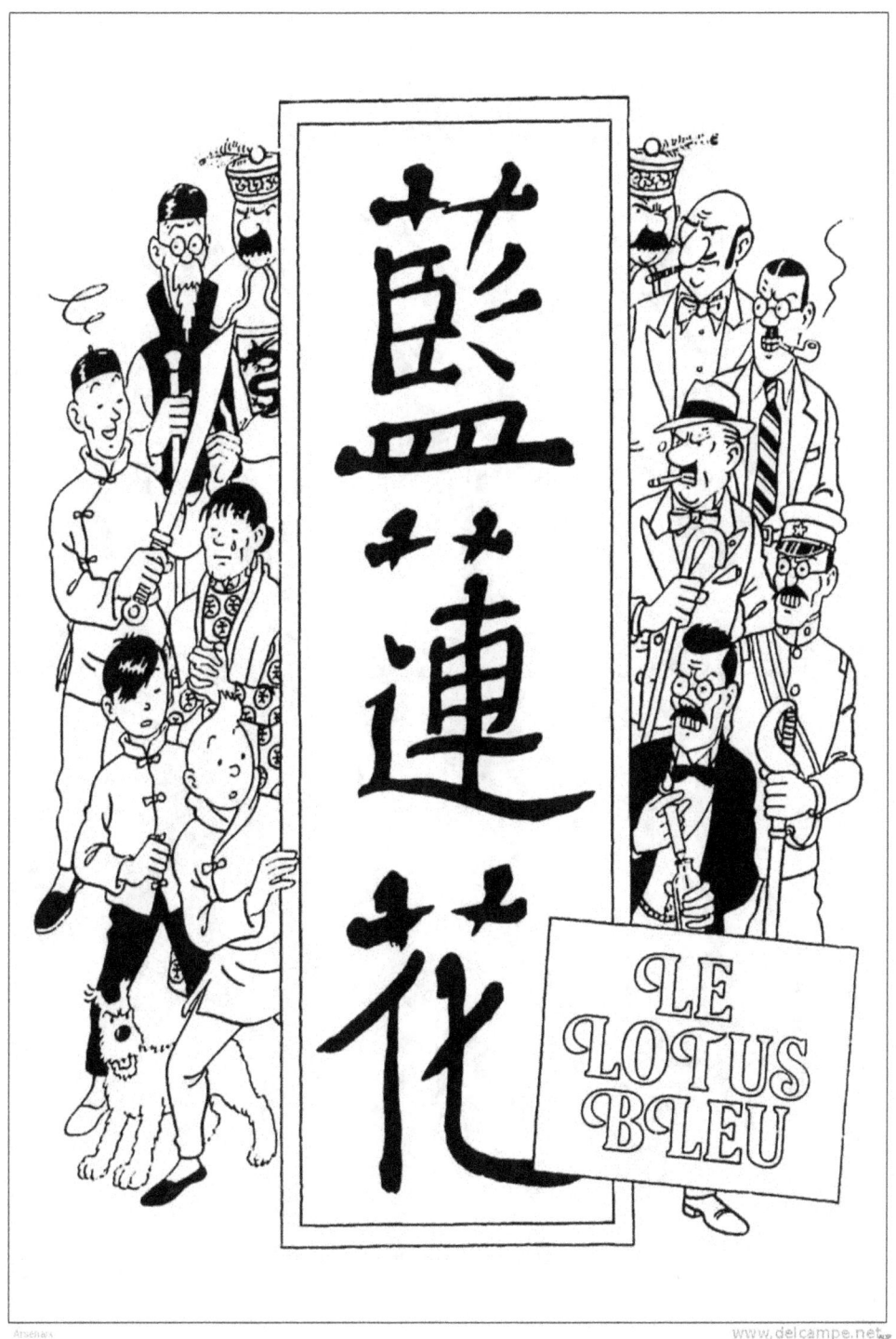

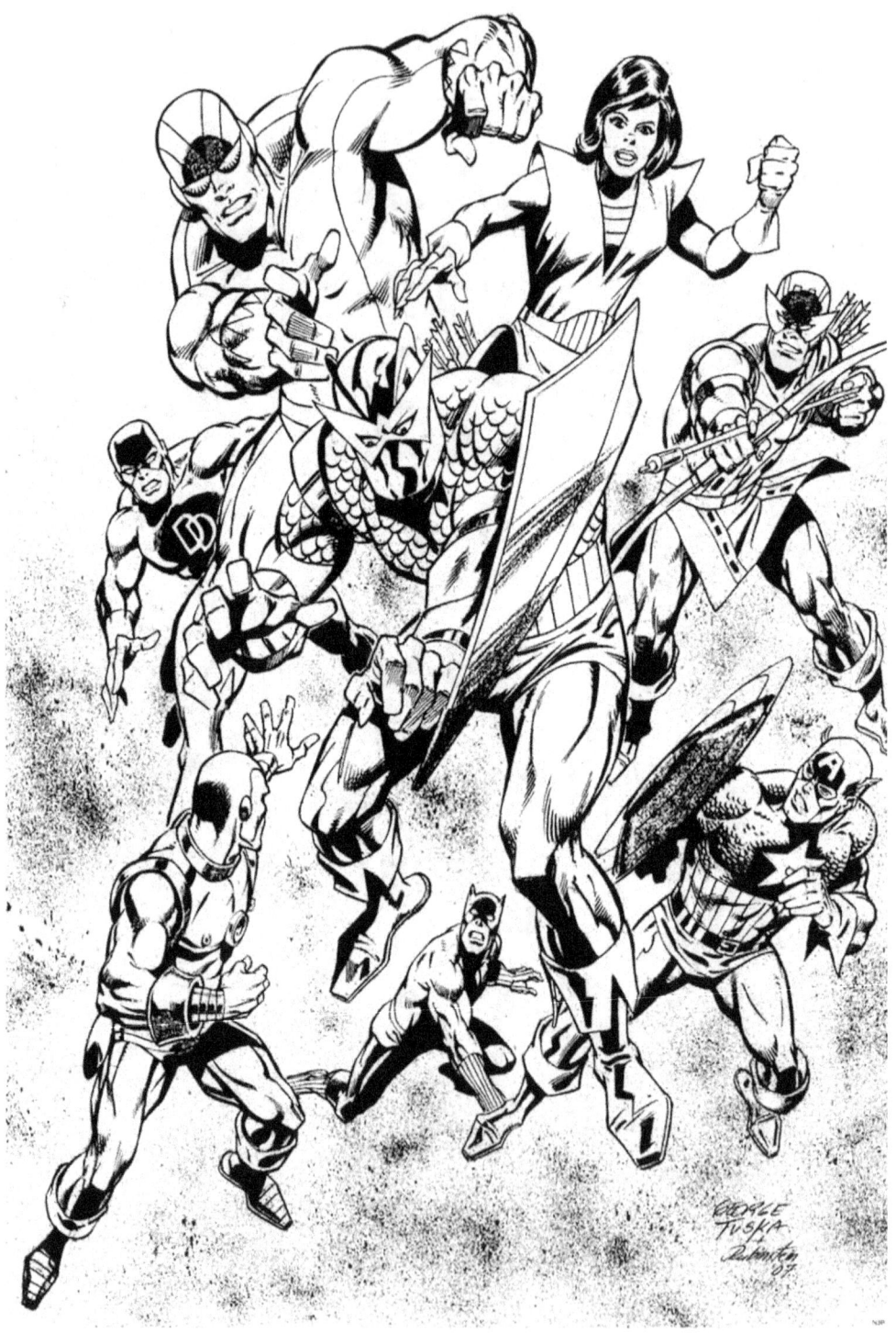

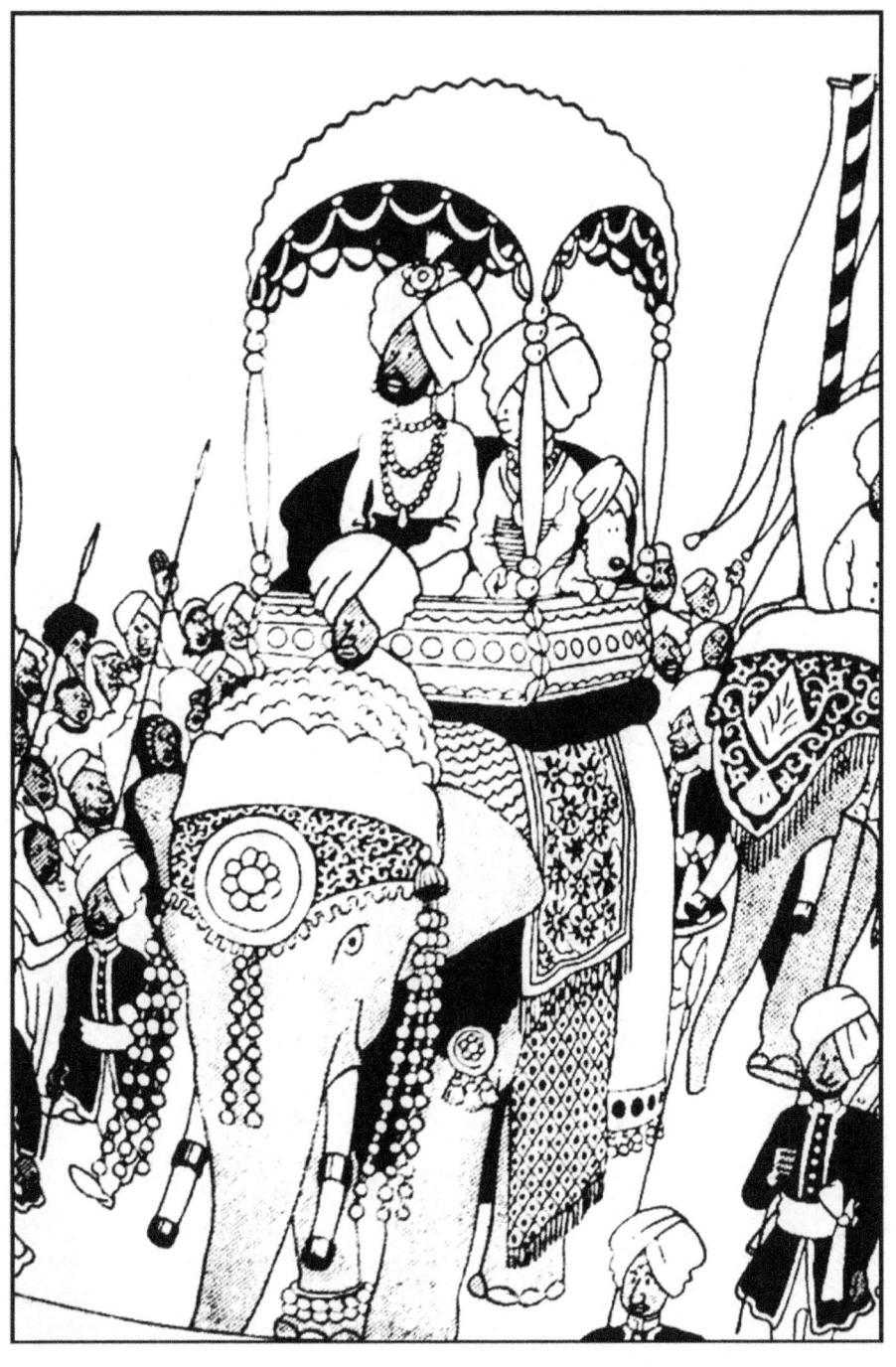

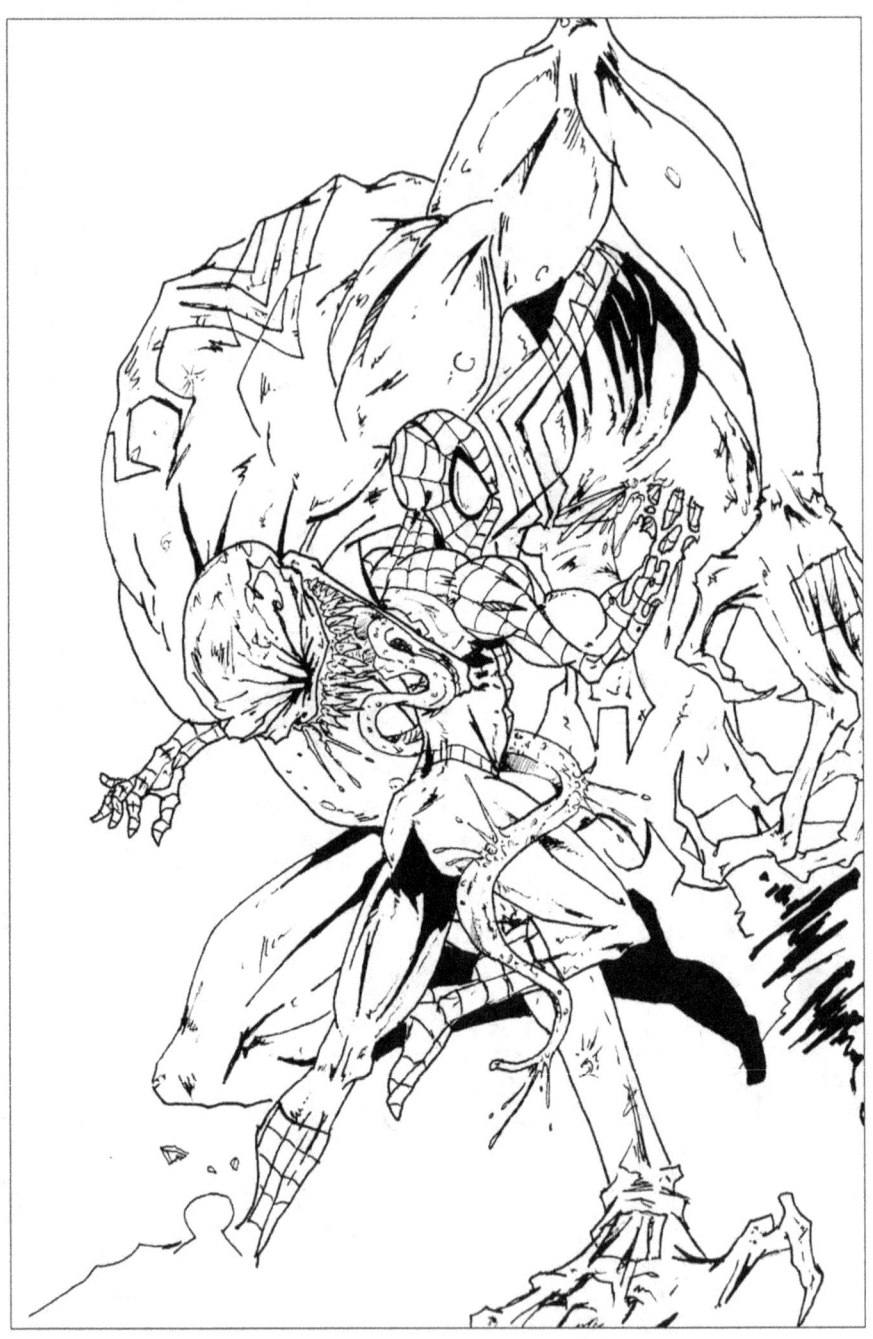

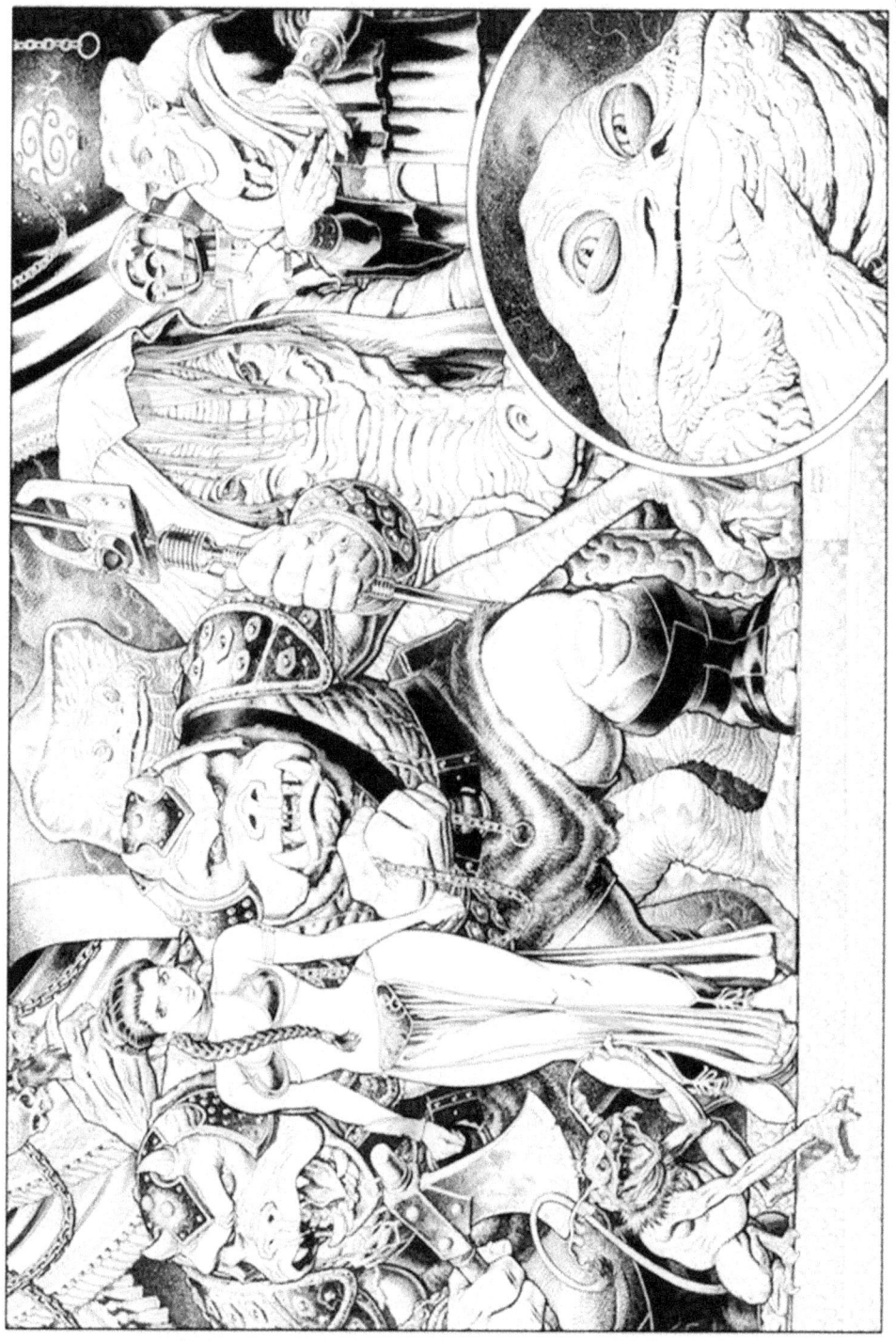

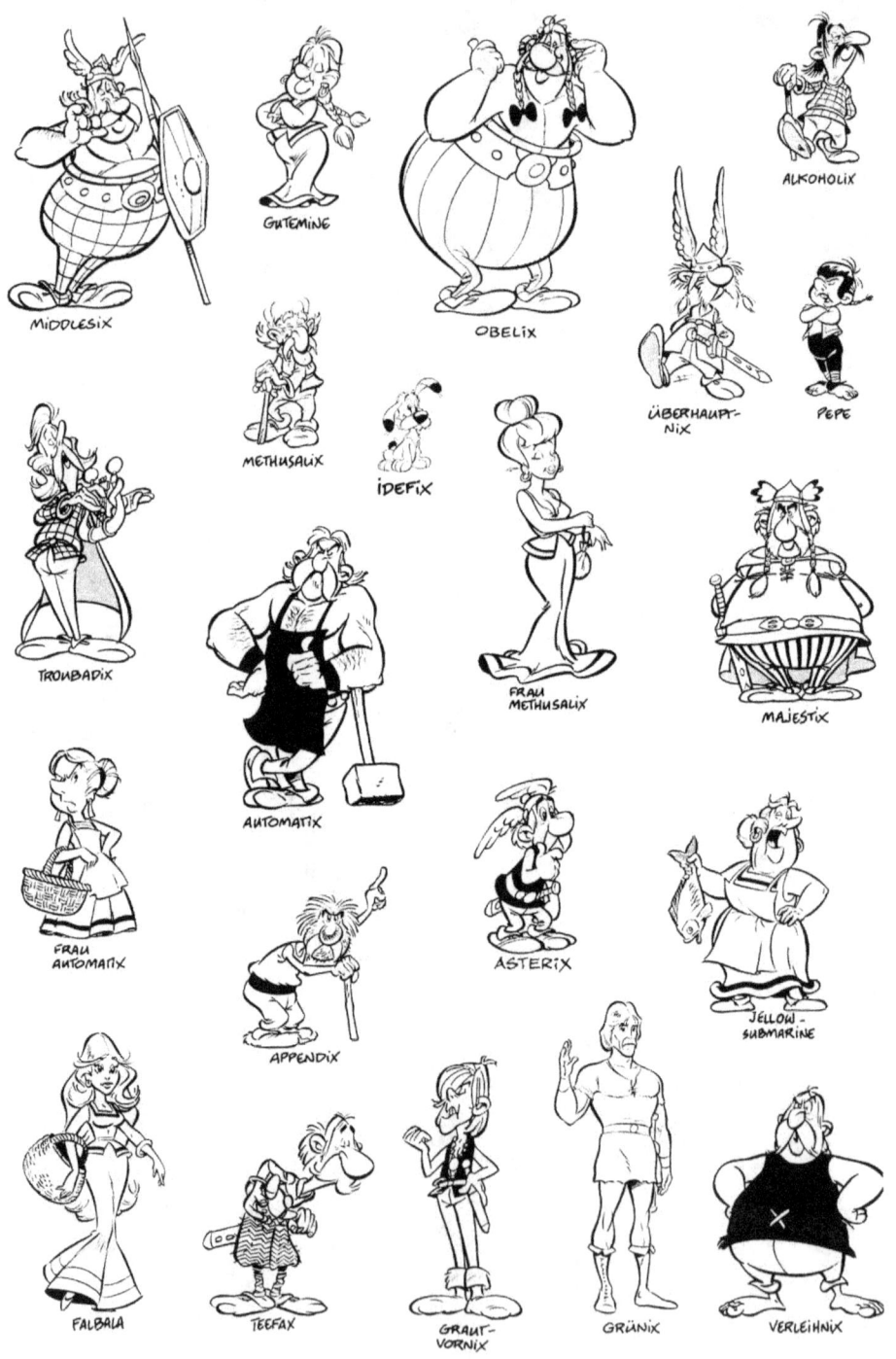

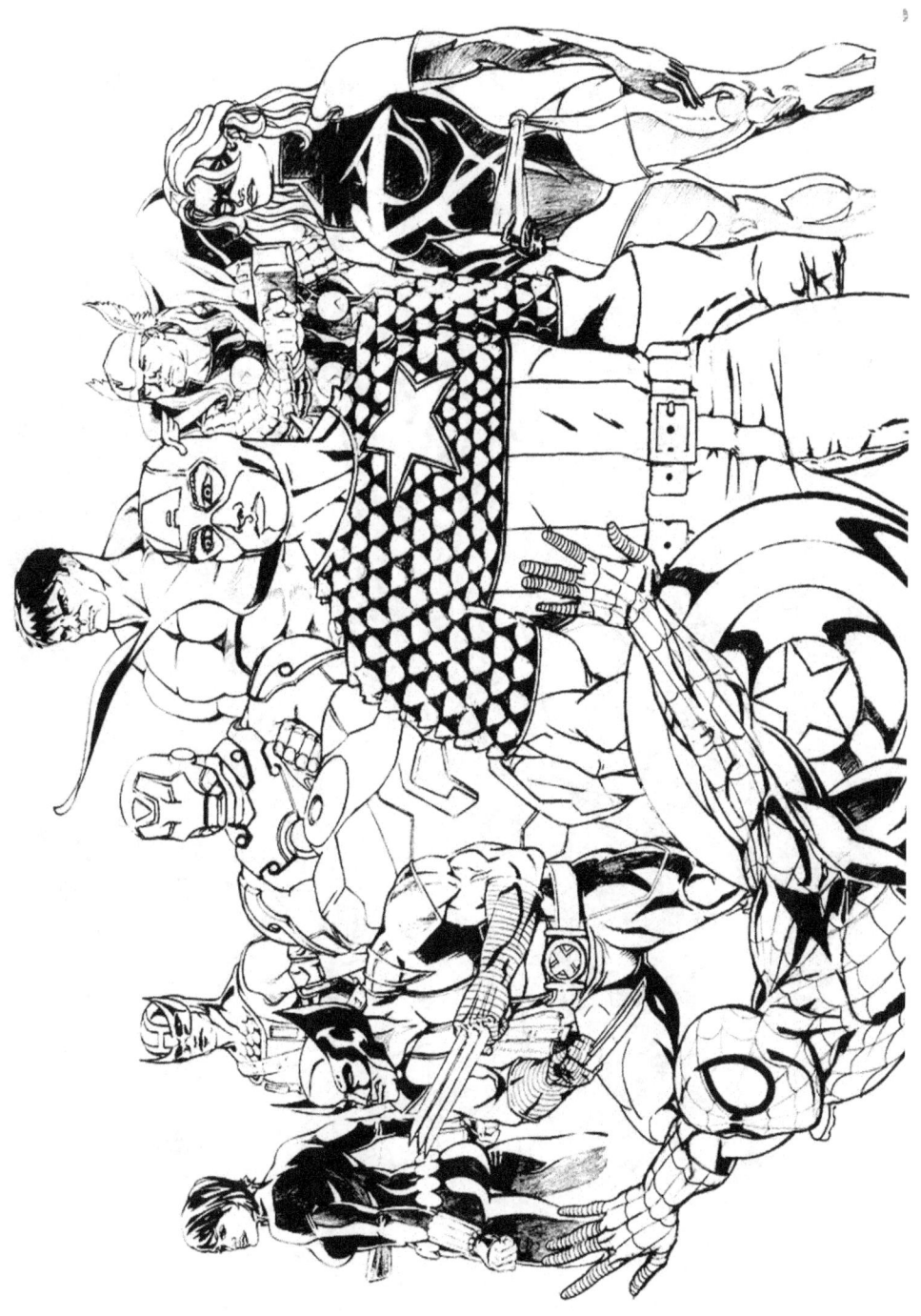

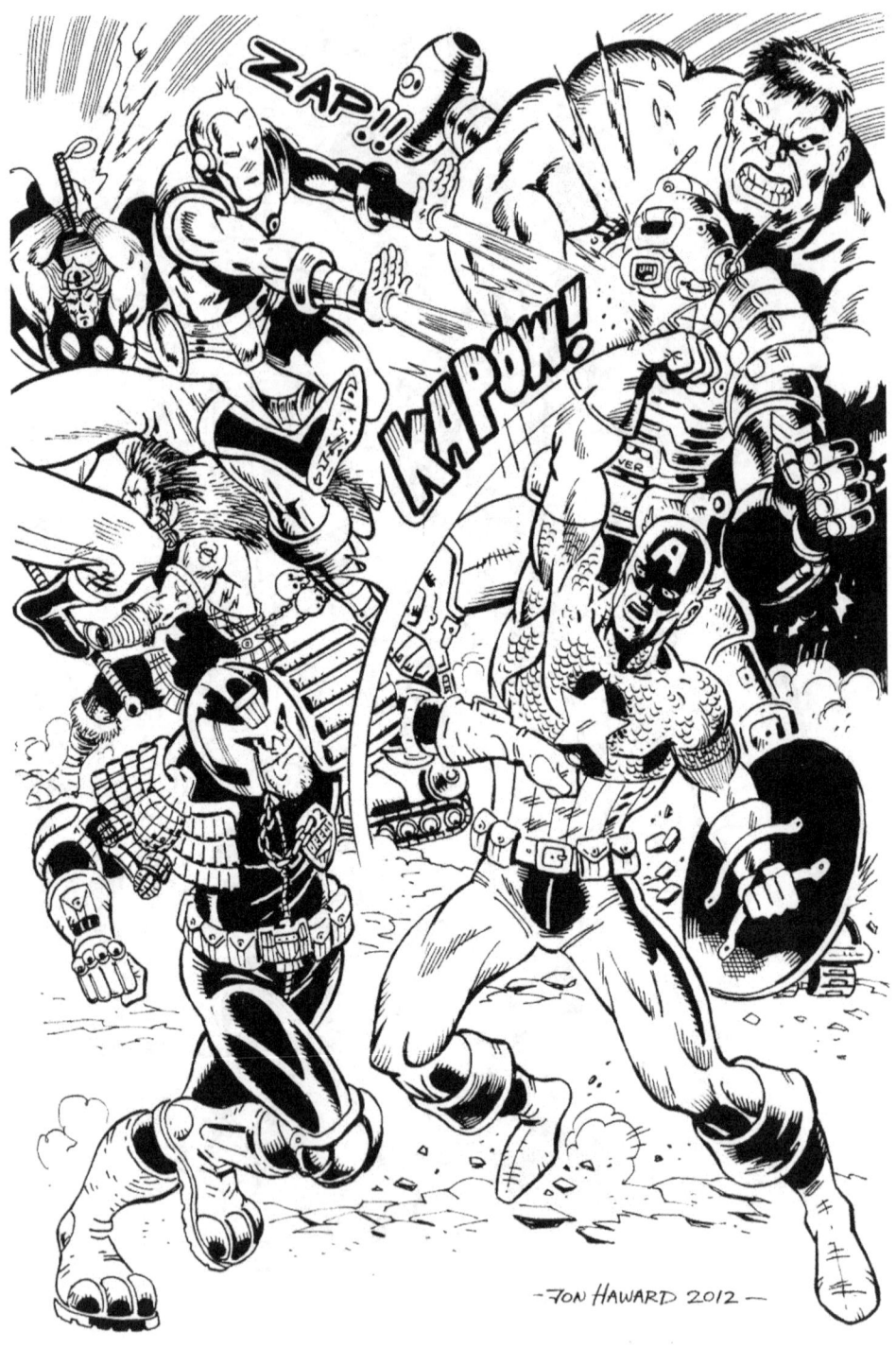

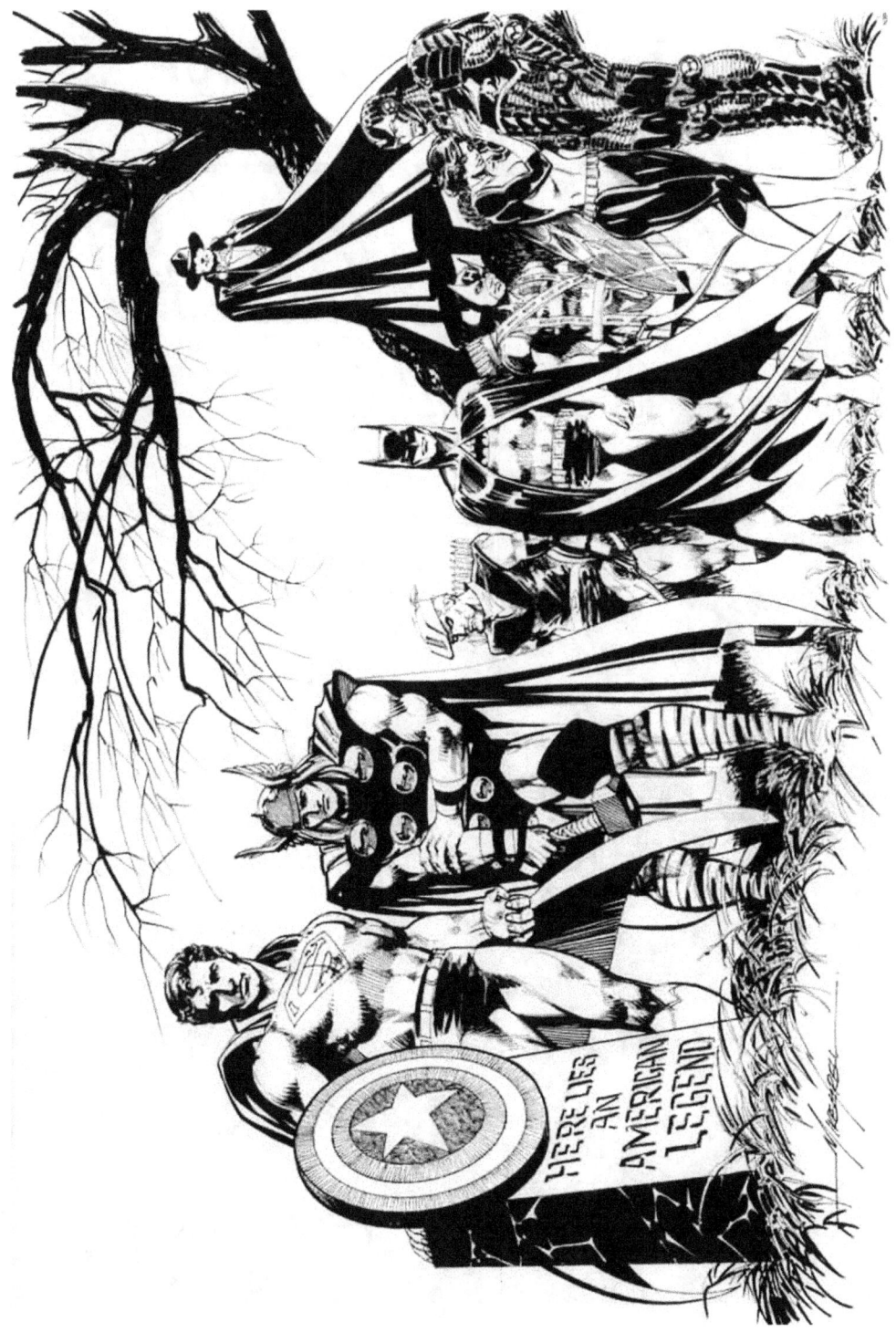

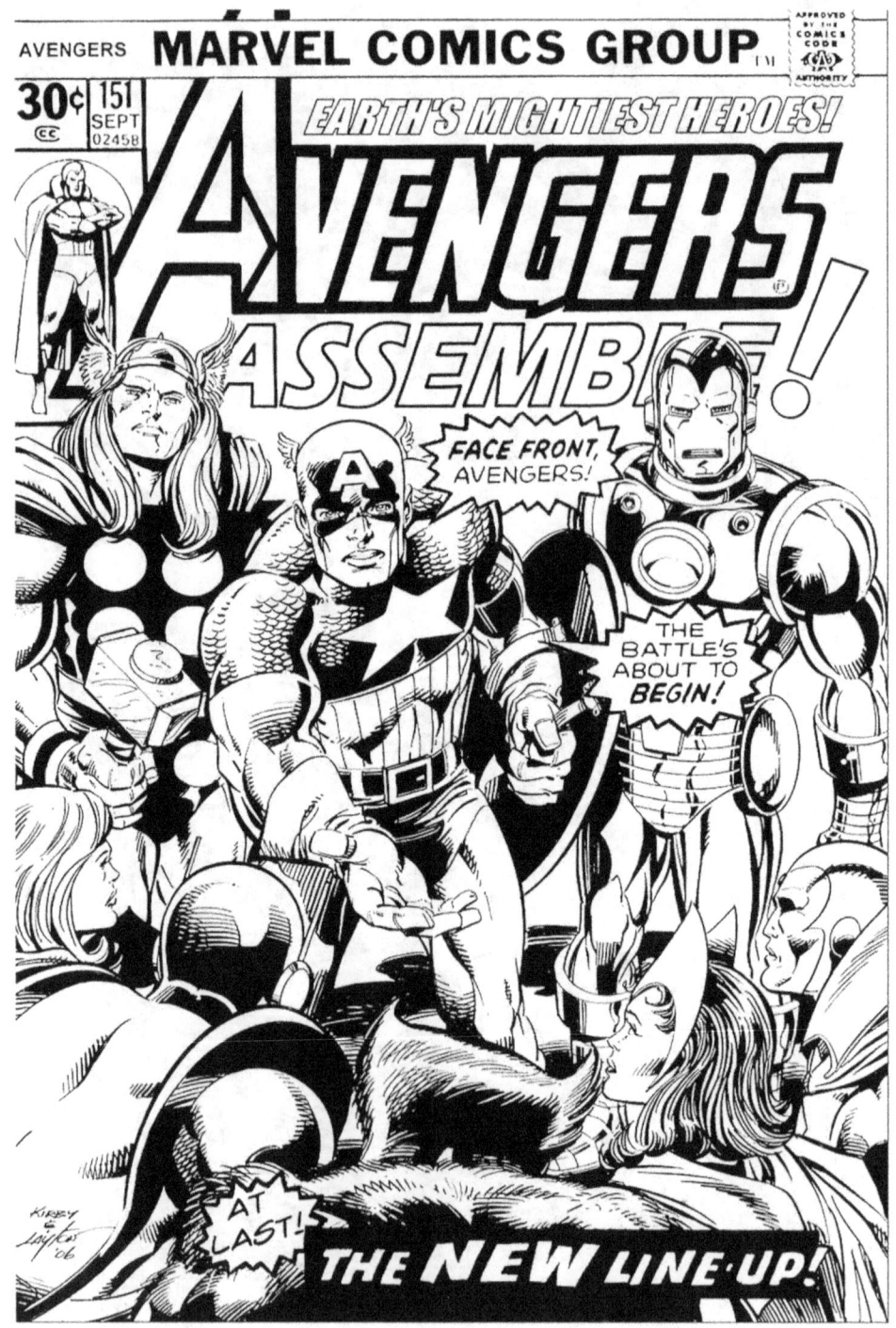

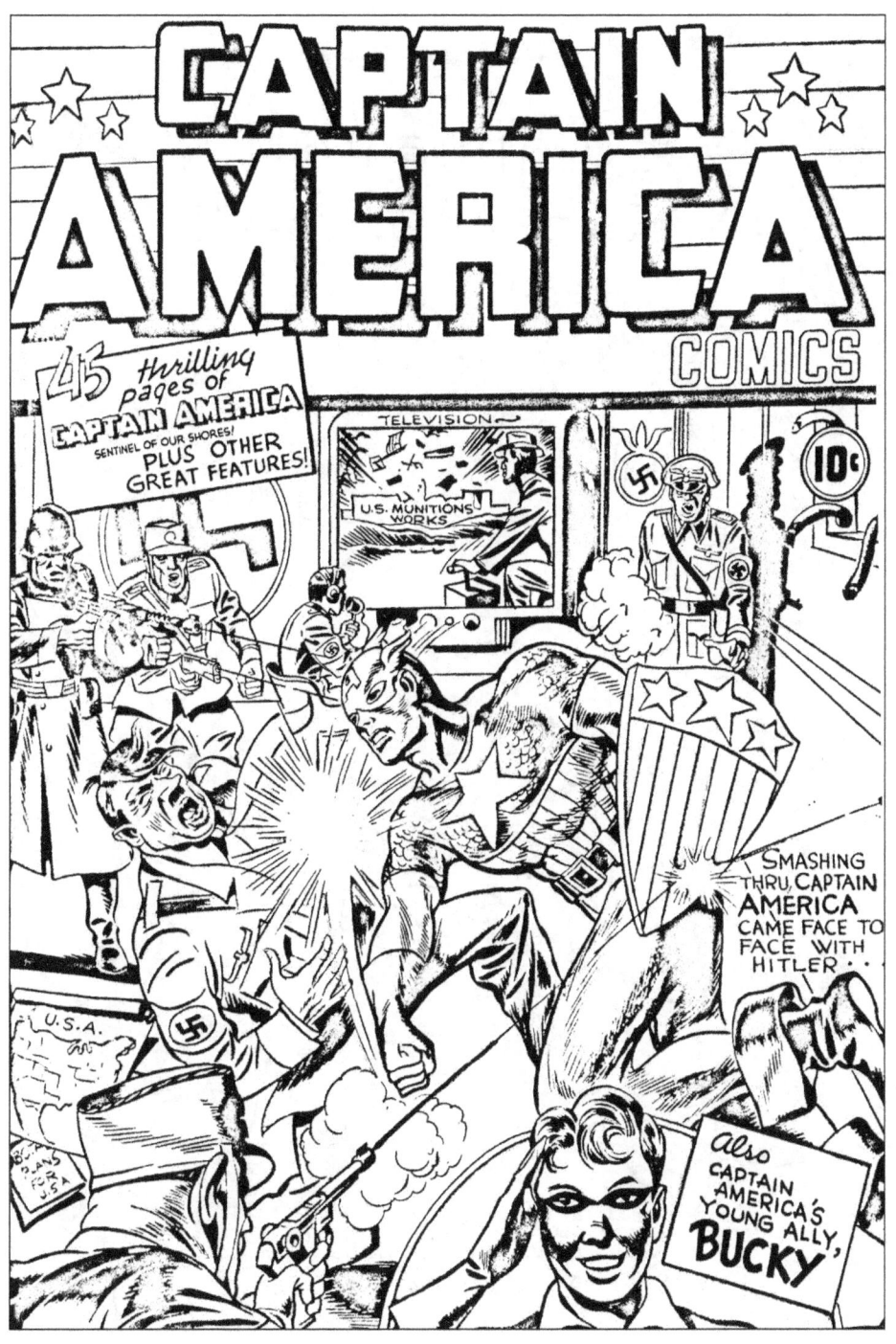

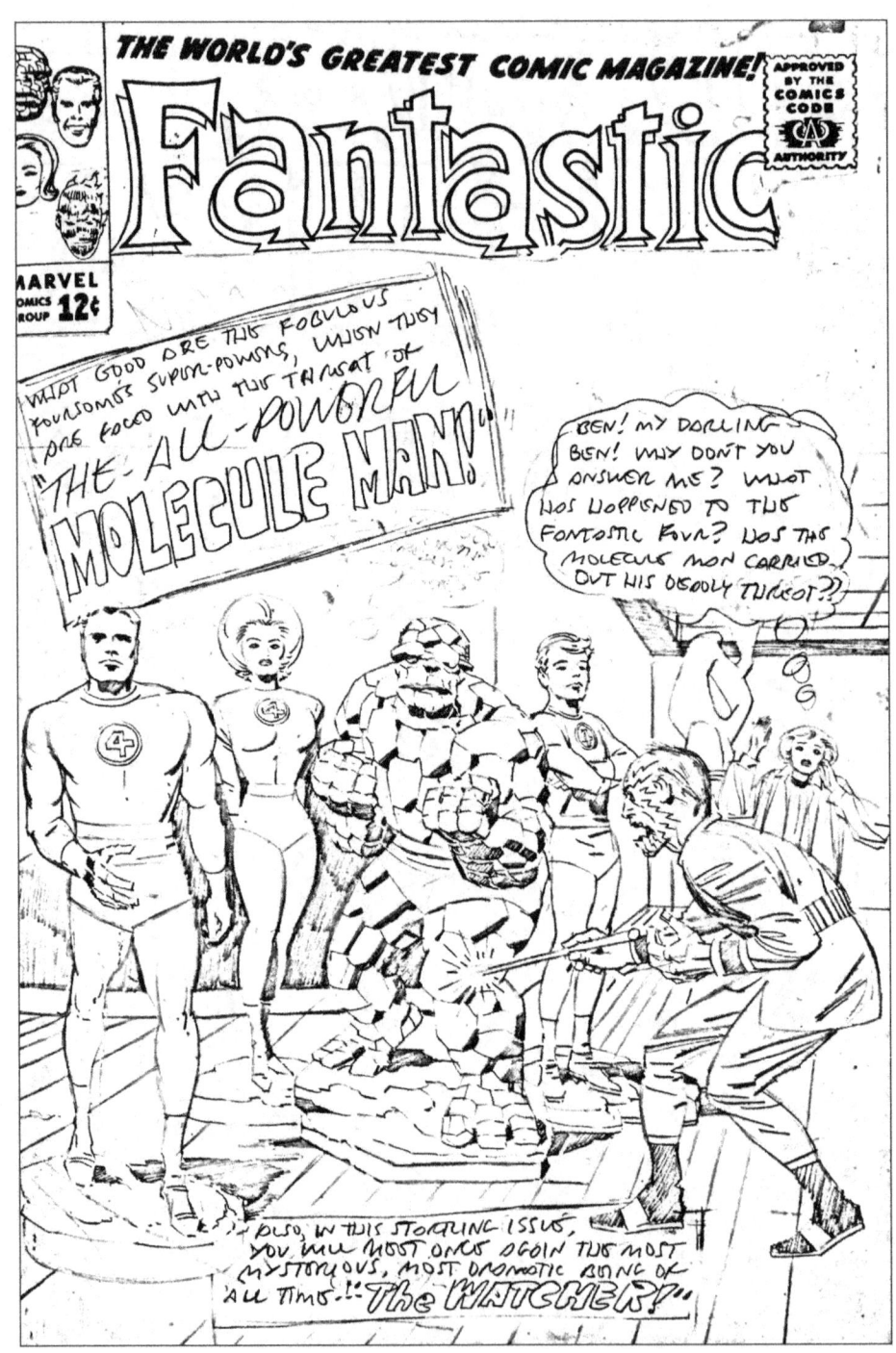

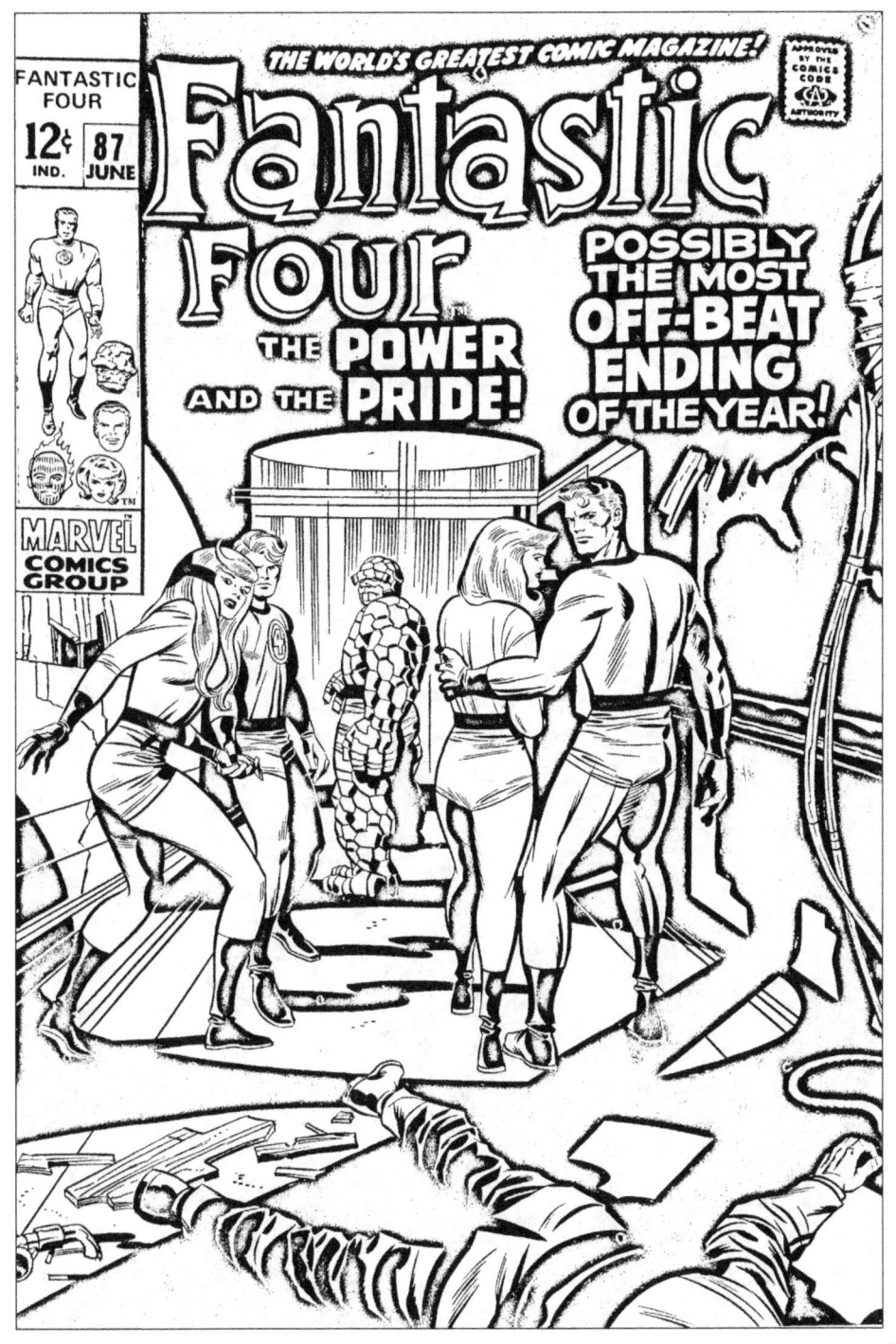

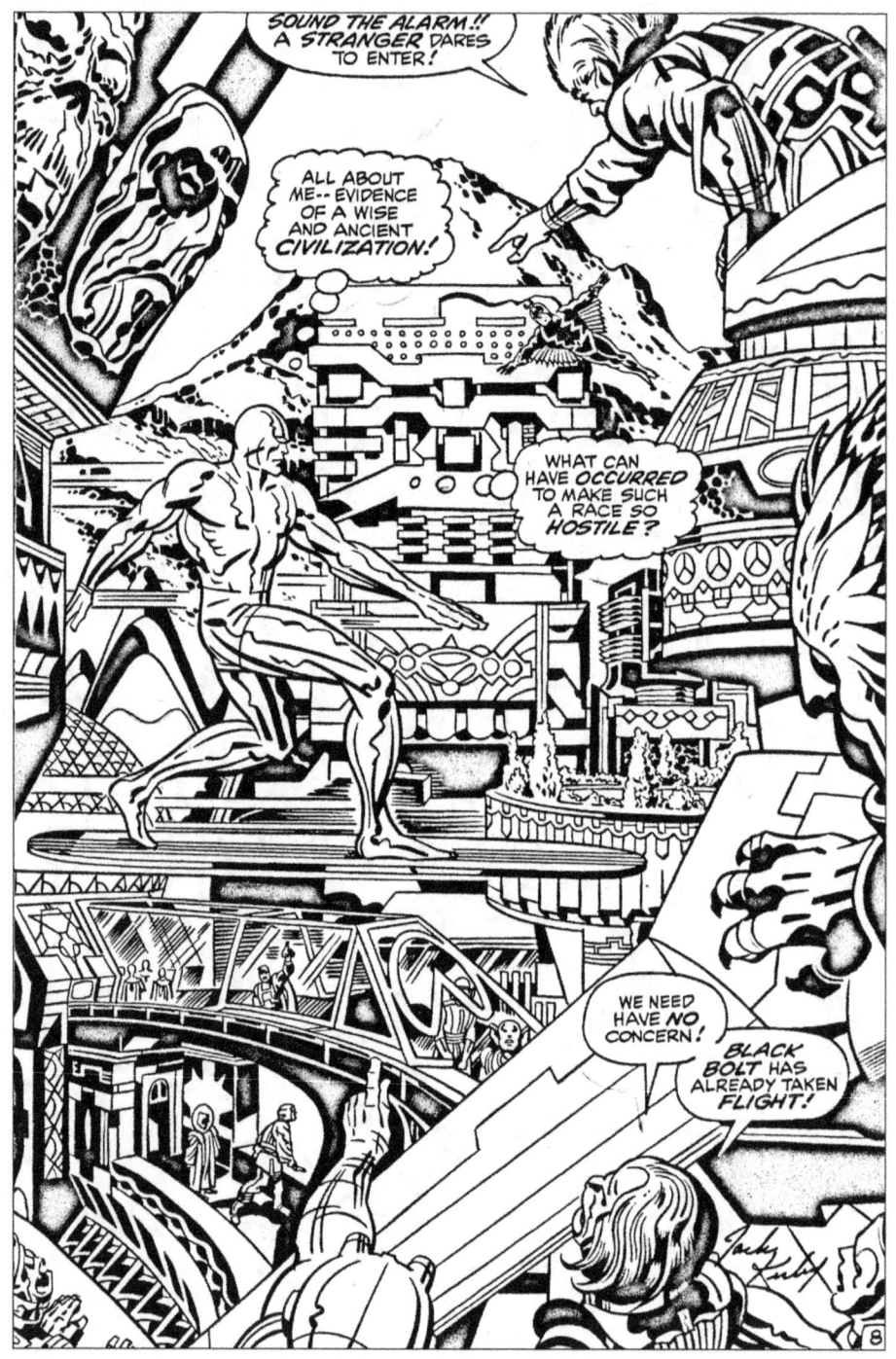

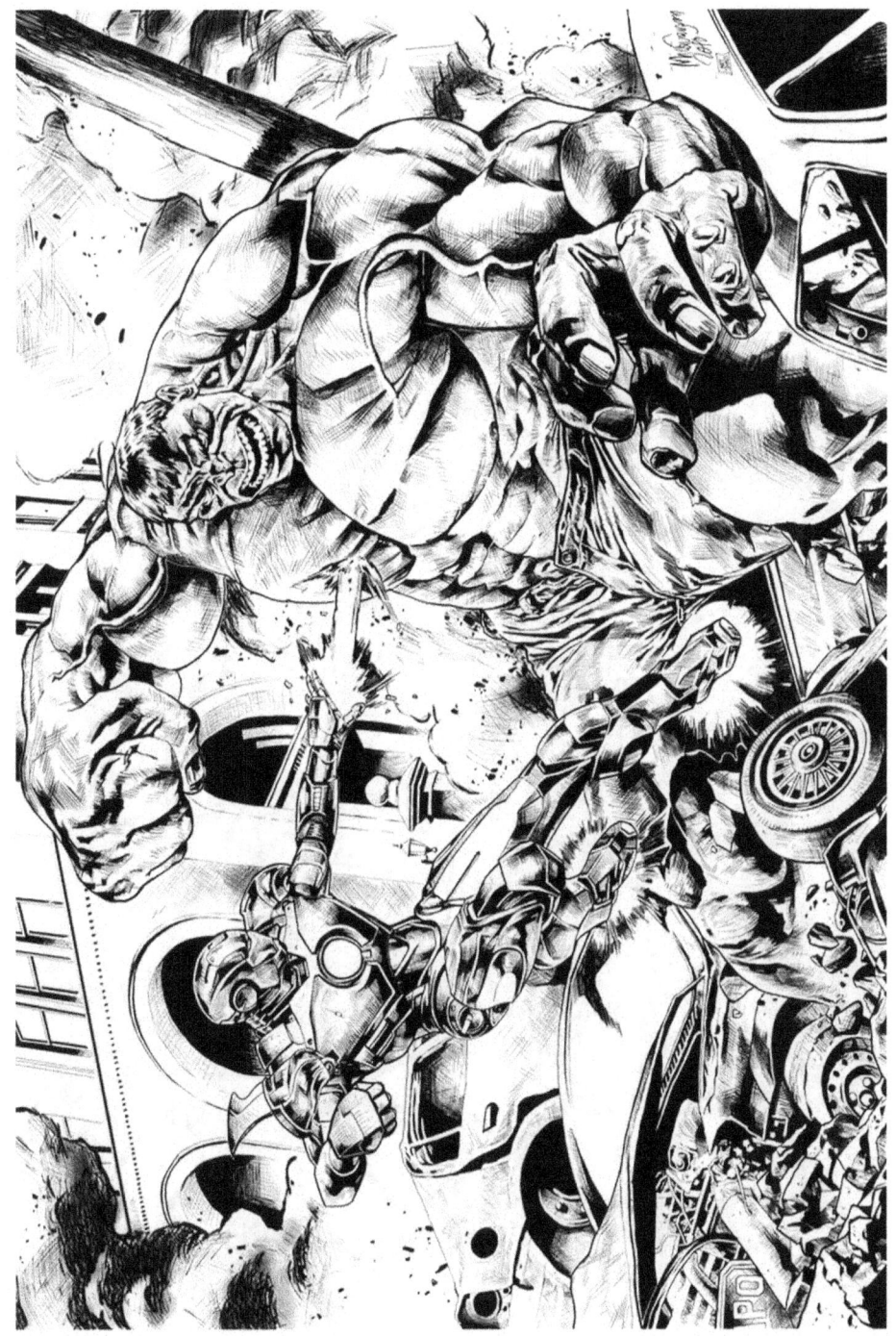

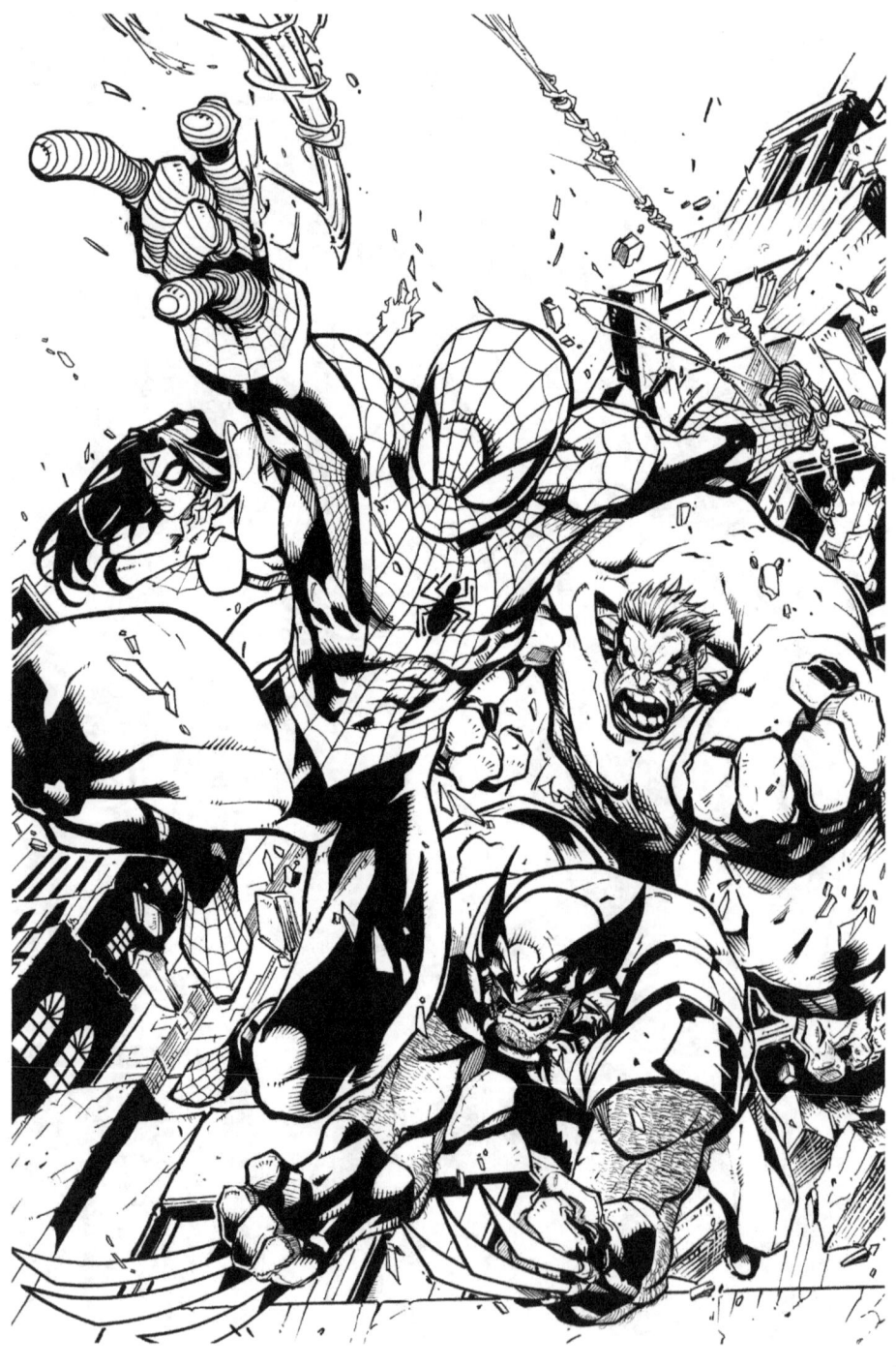

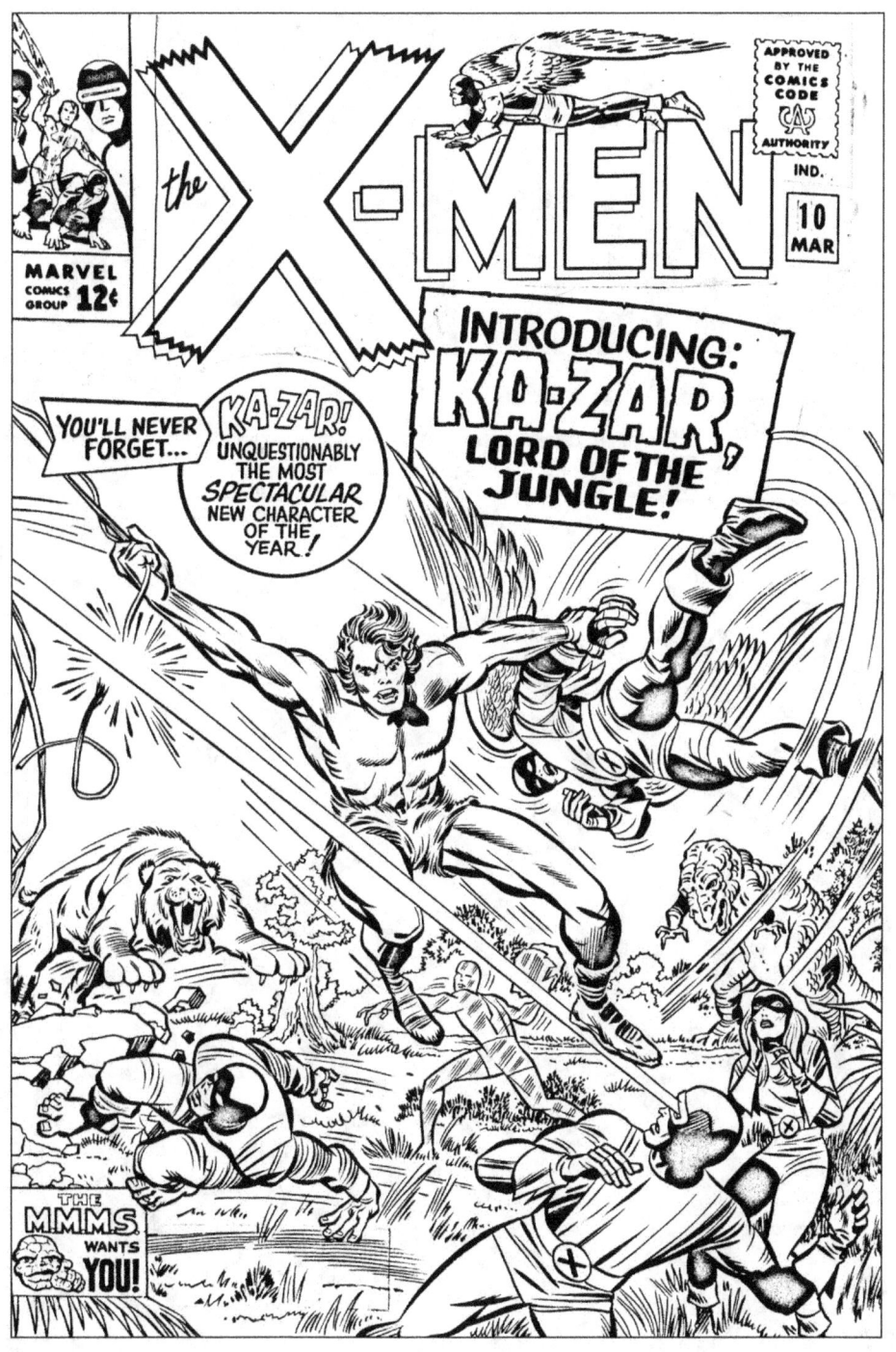

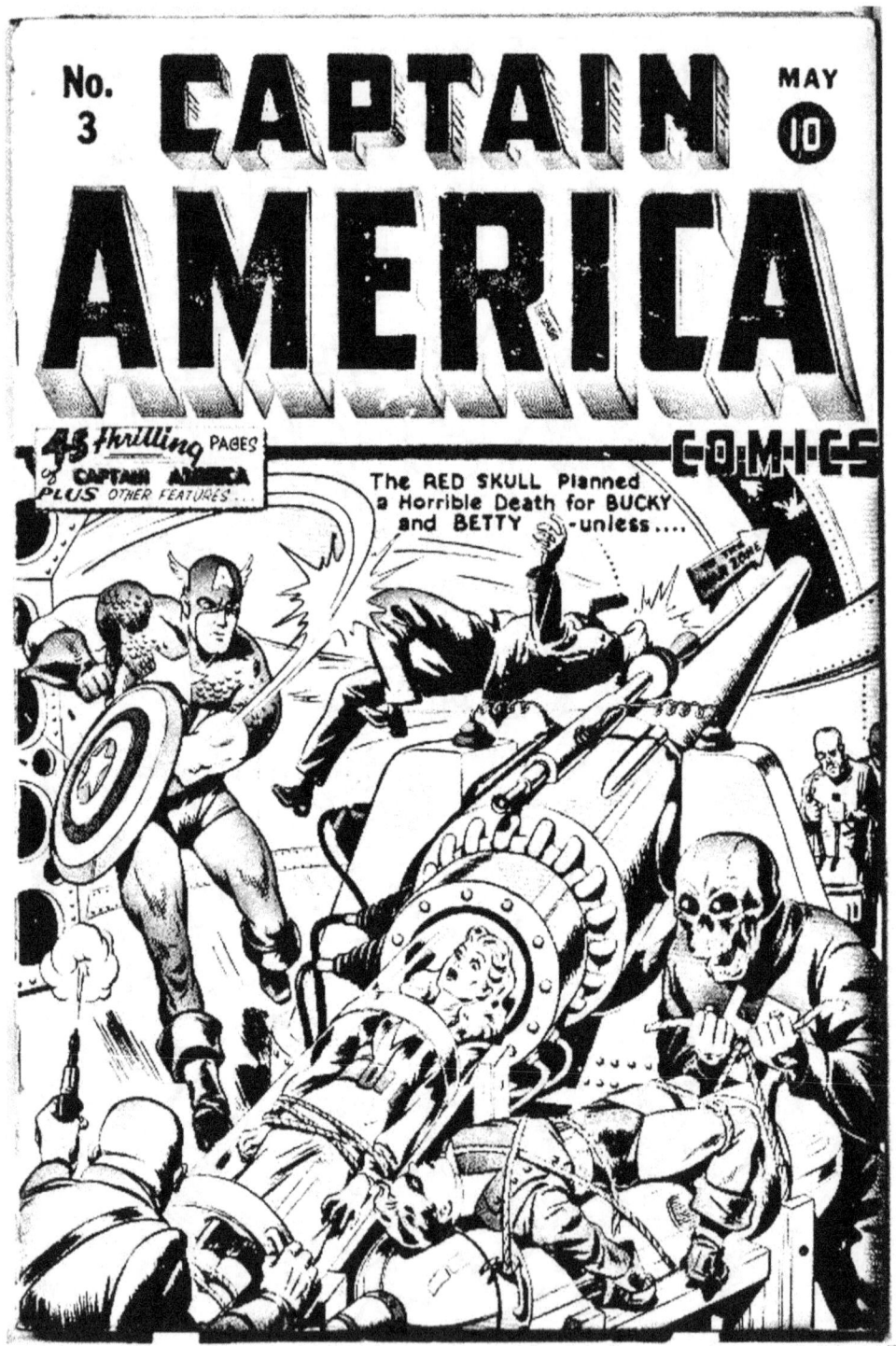

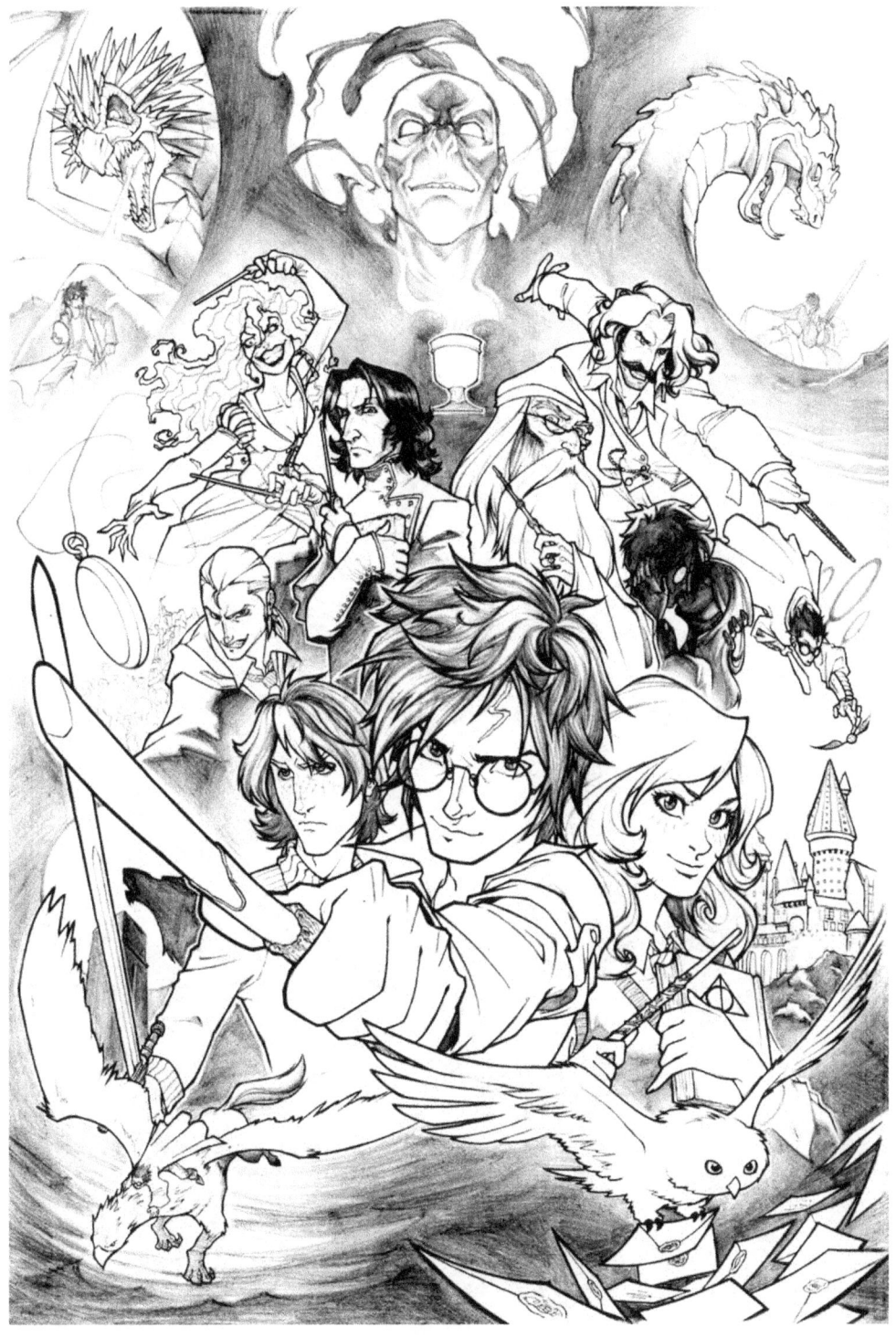

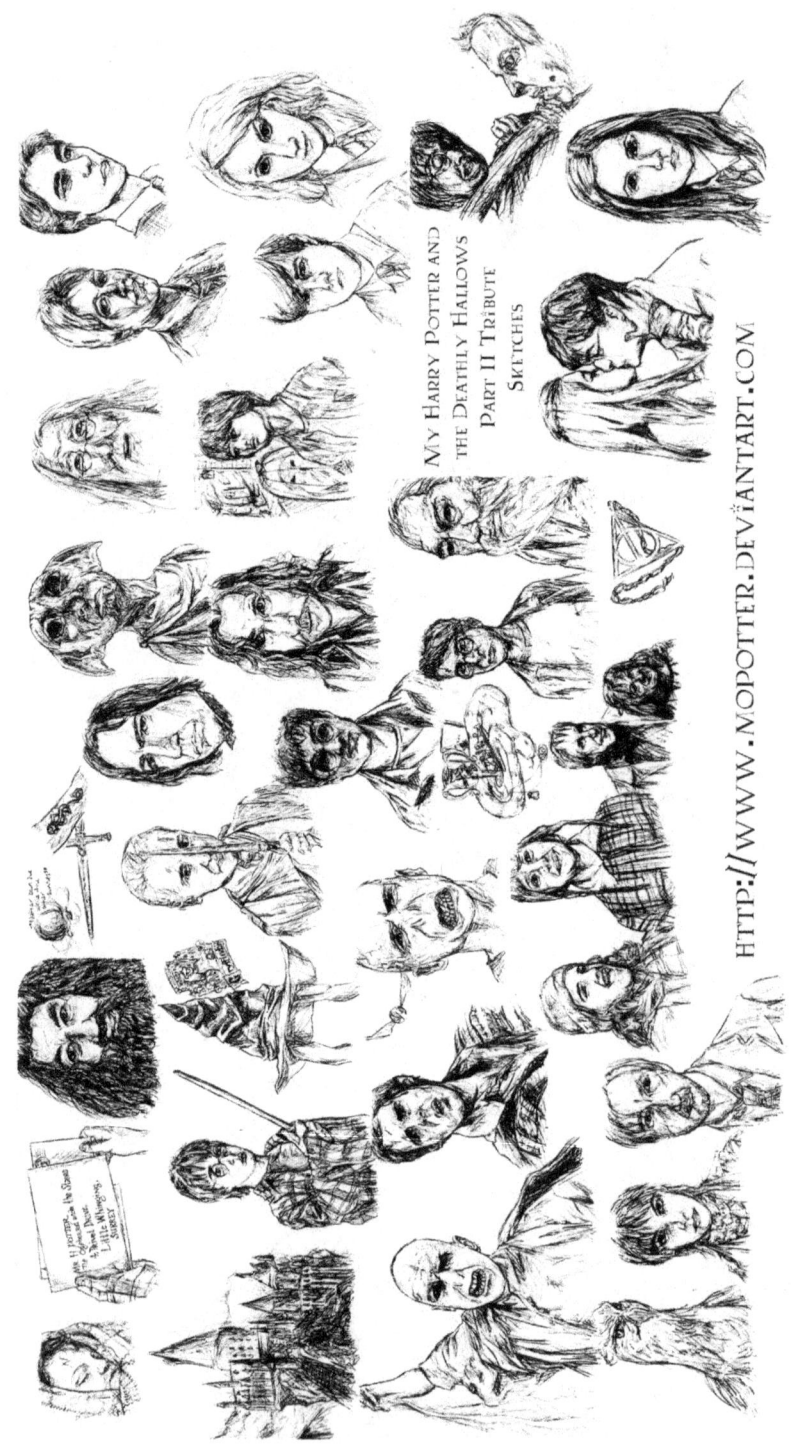

My Harry Potter and the Deathly Hallows Part II Tribute Sketches

HTTP://WWW.MOPOTTER.DEVIANTART.COM

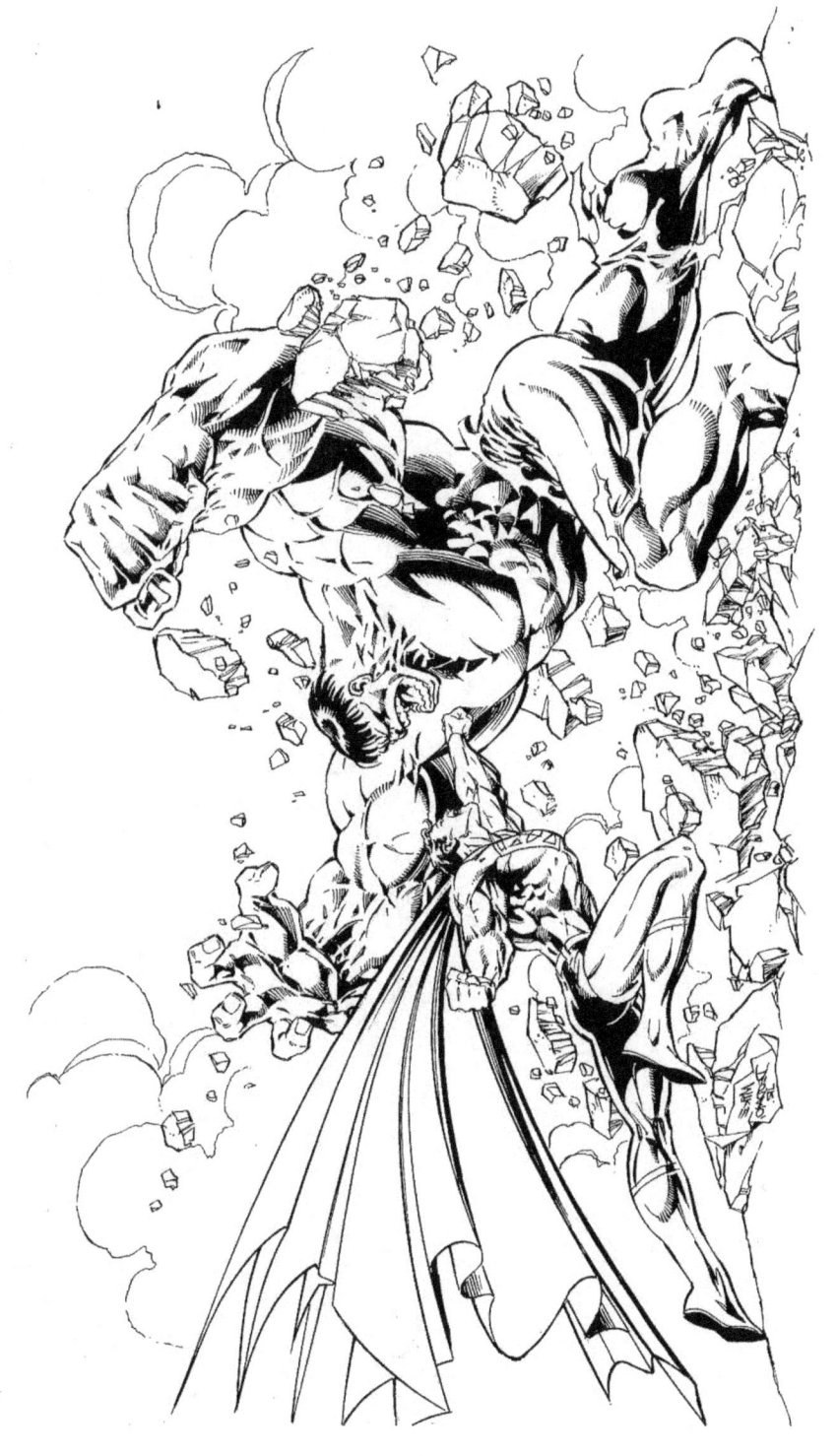

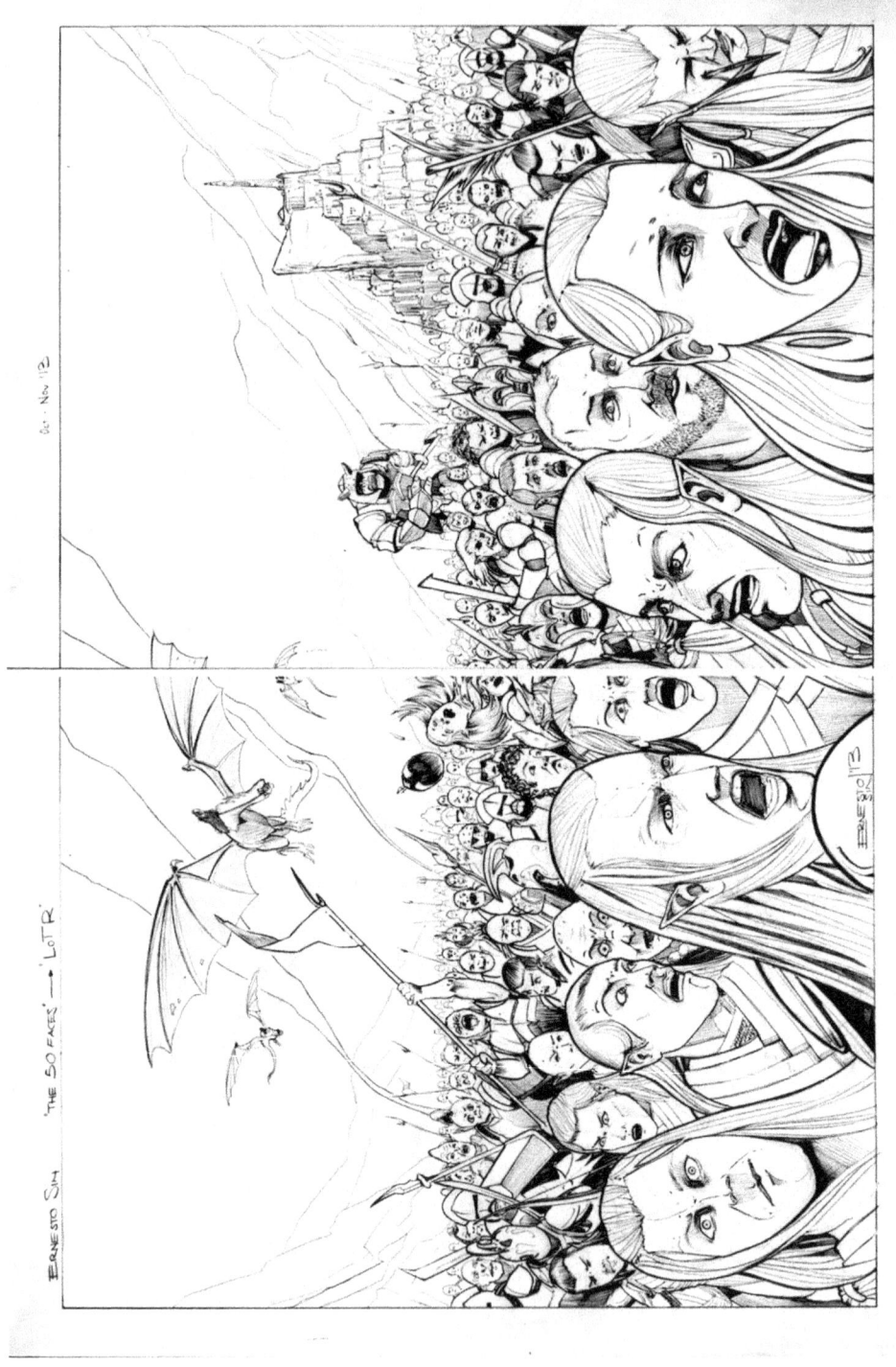

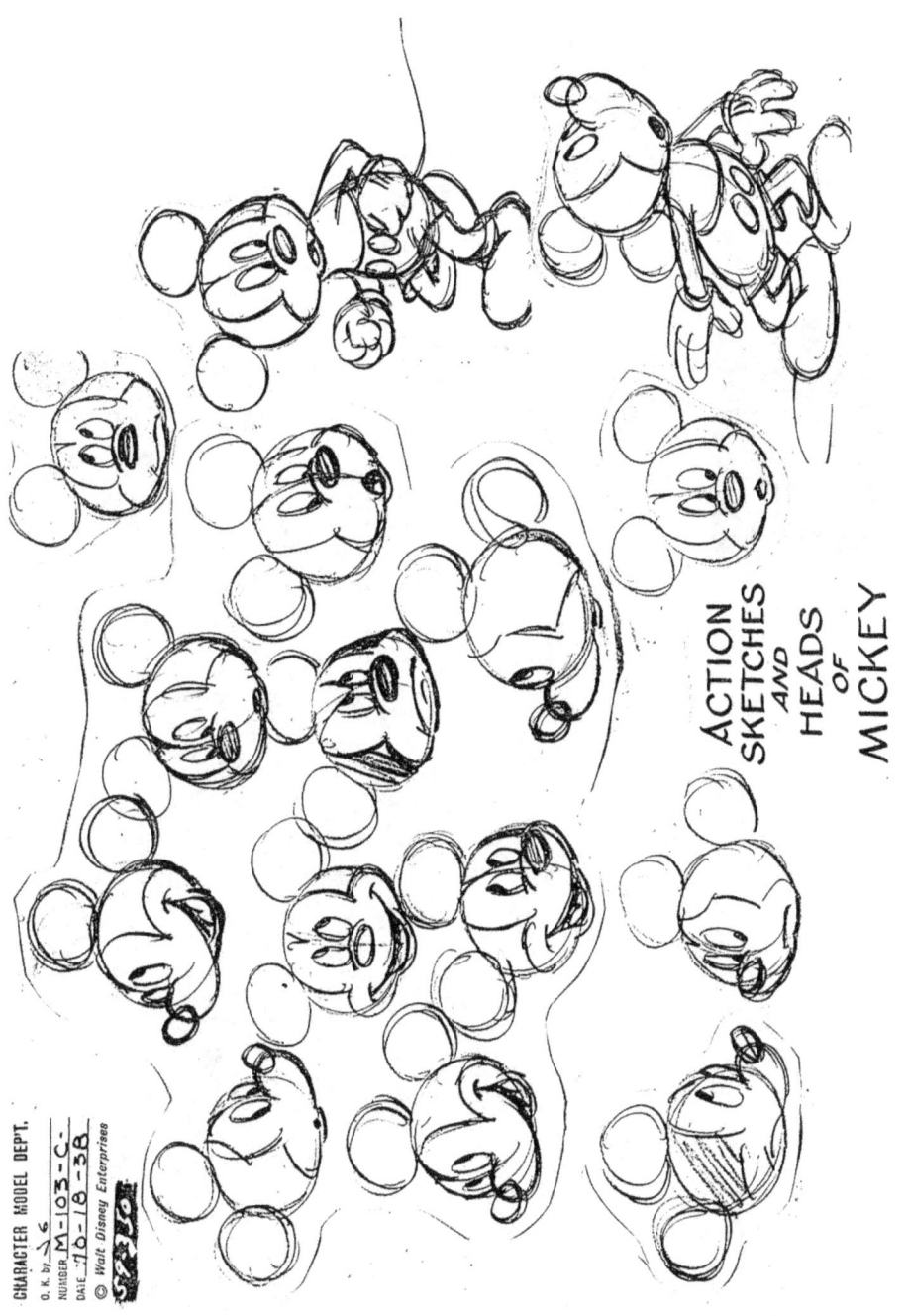

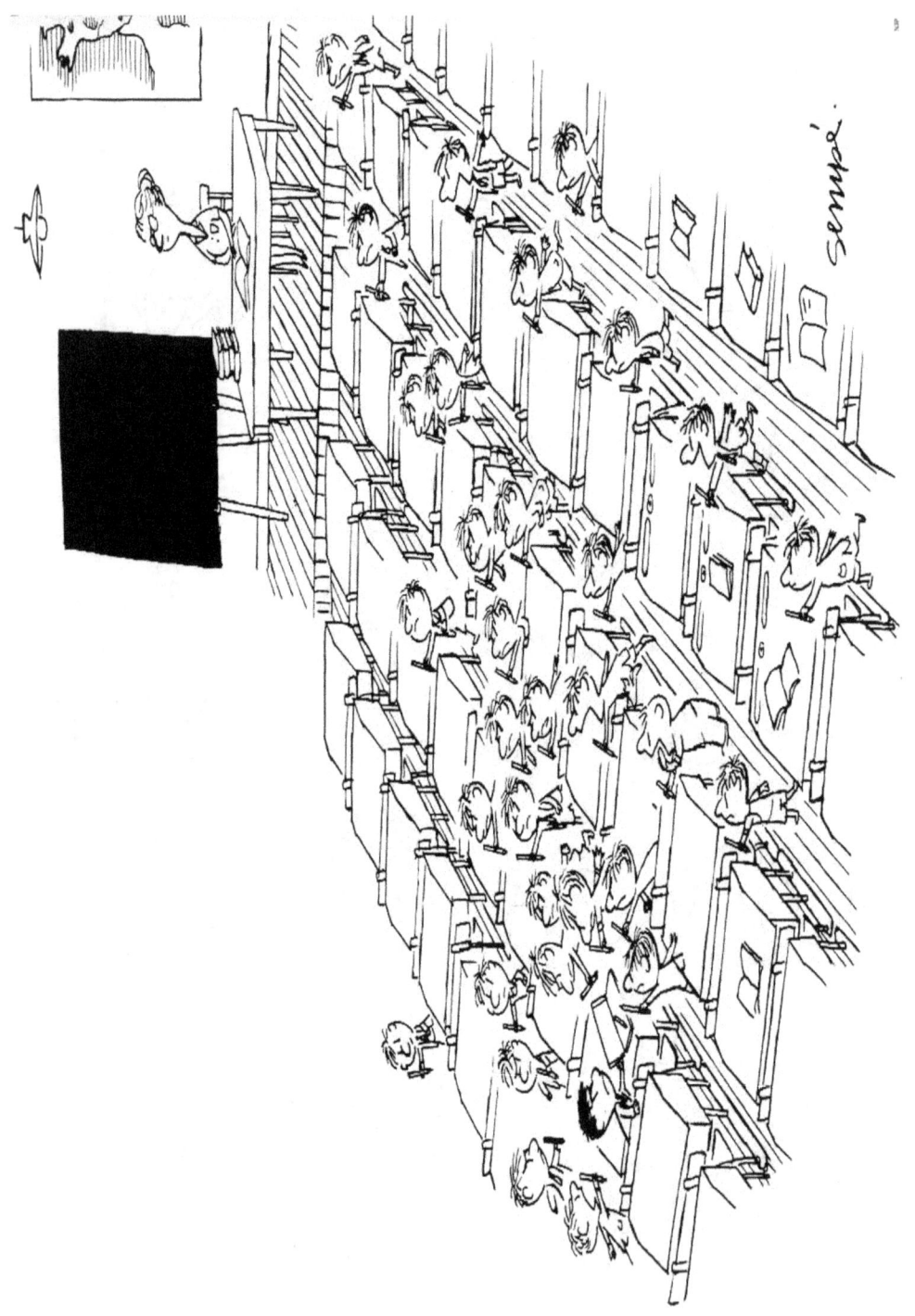

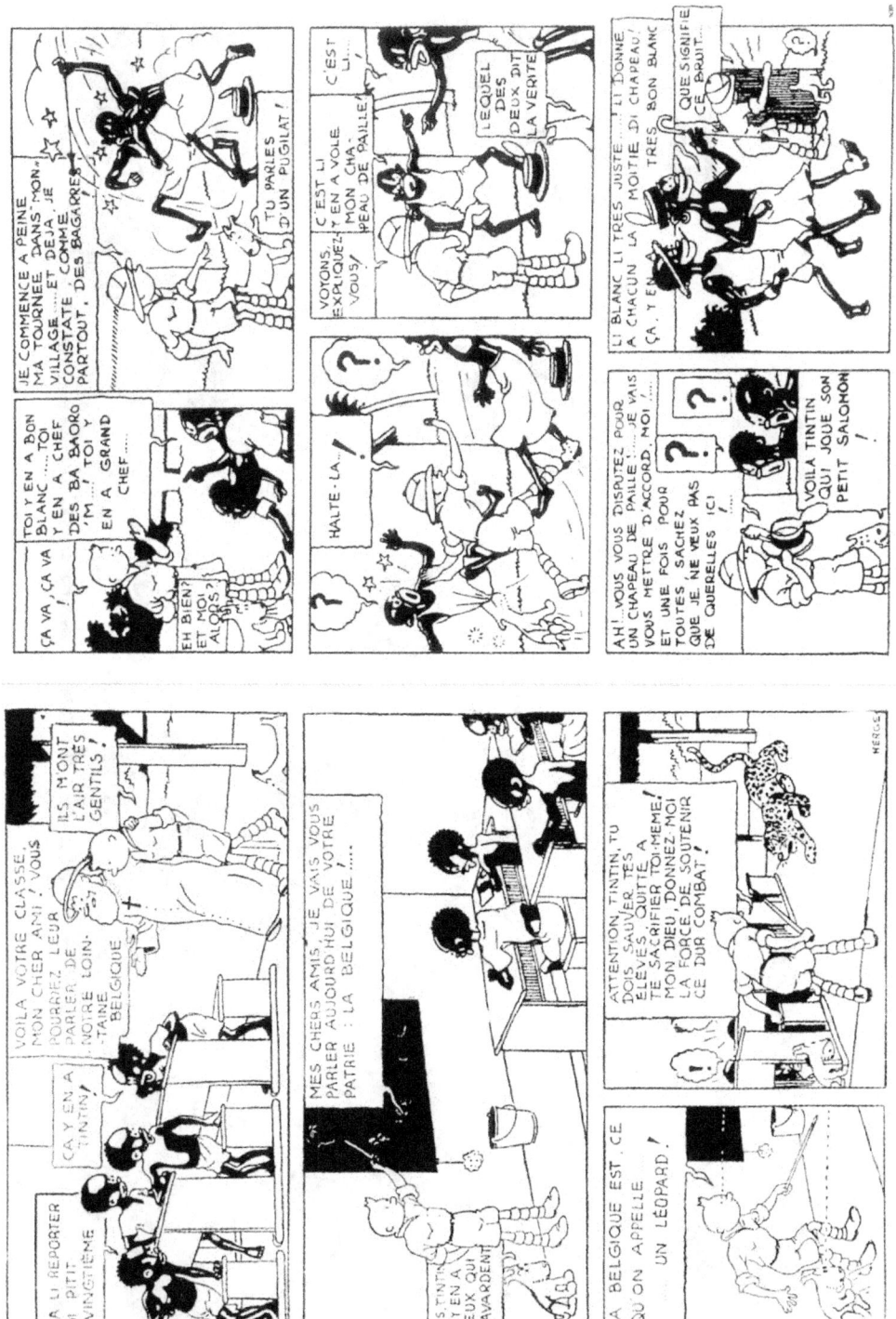

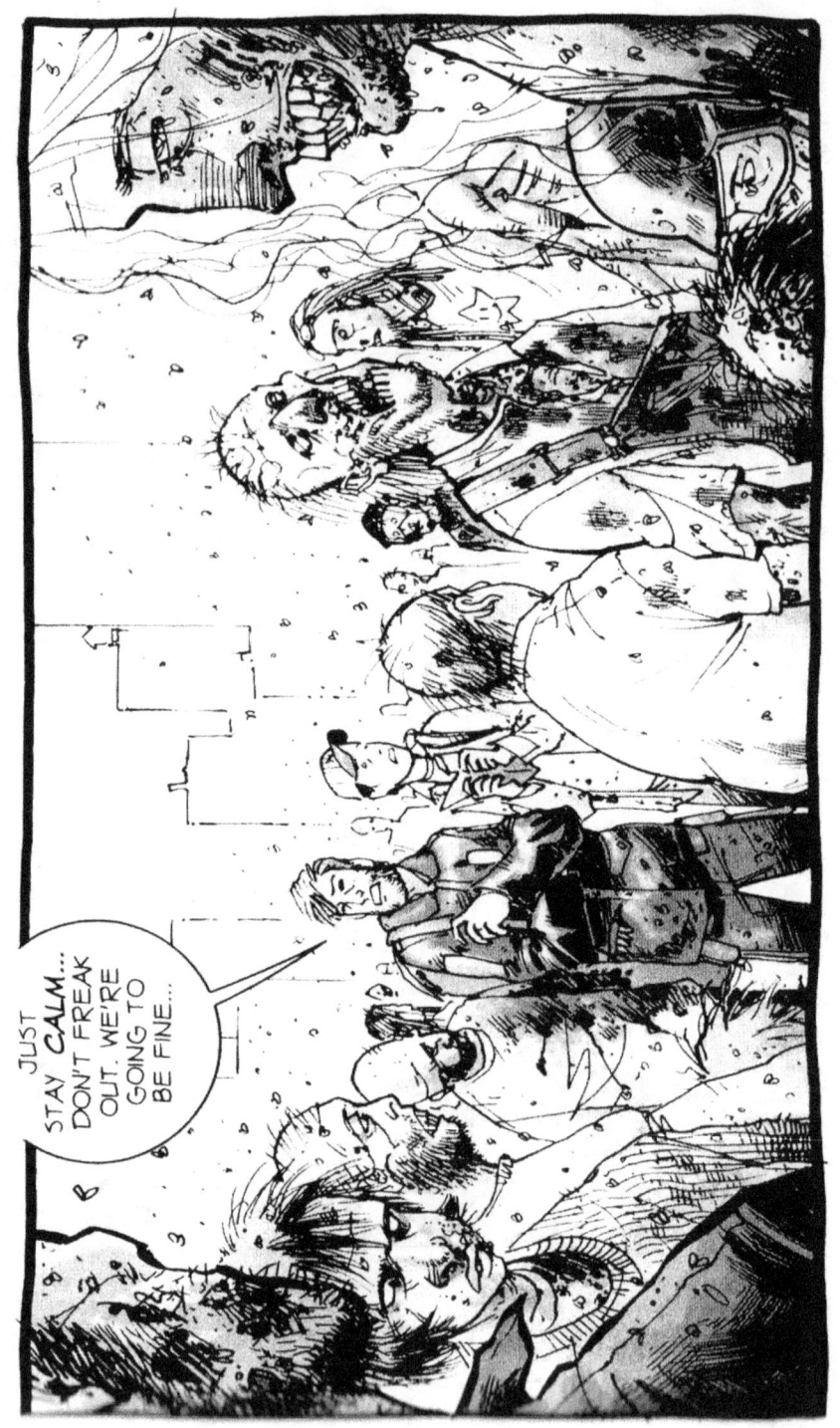

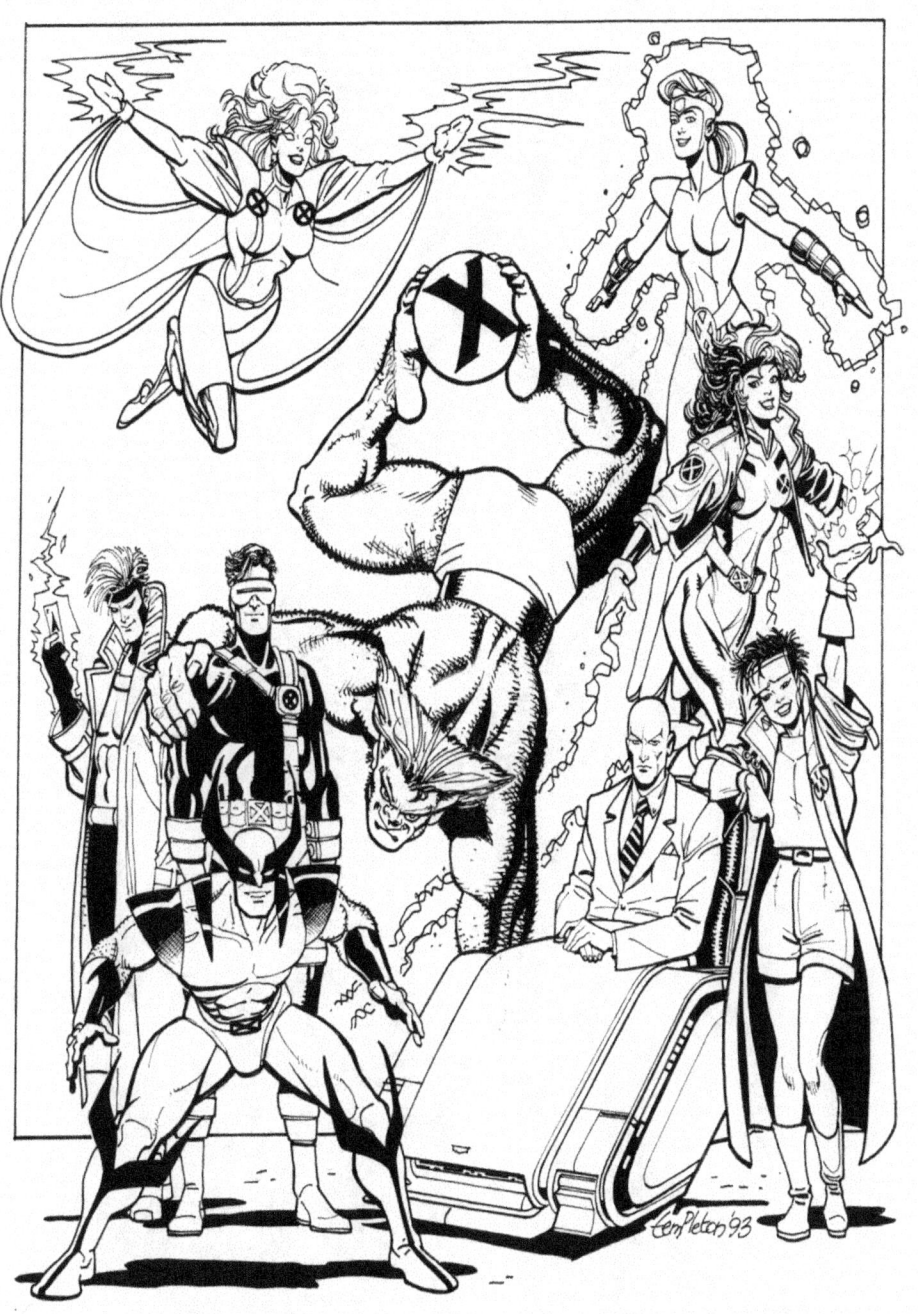

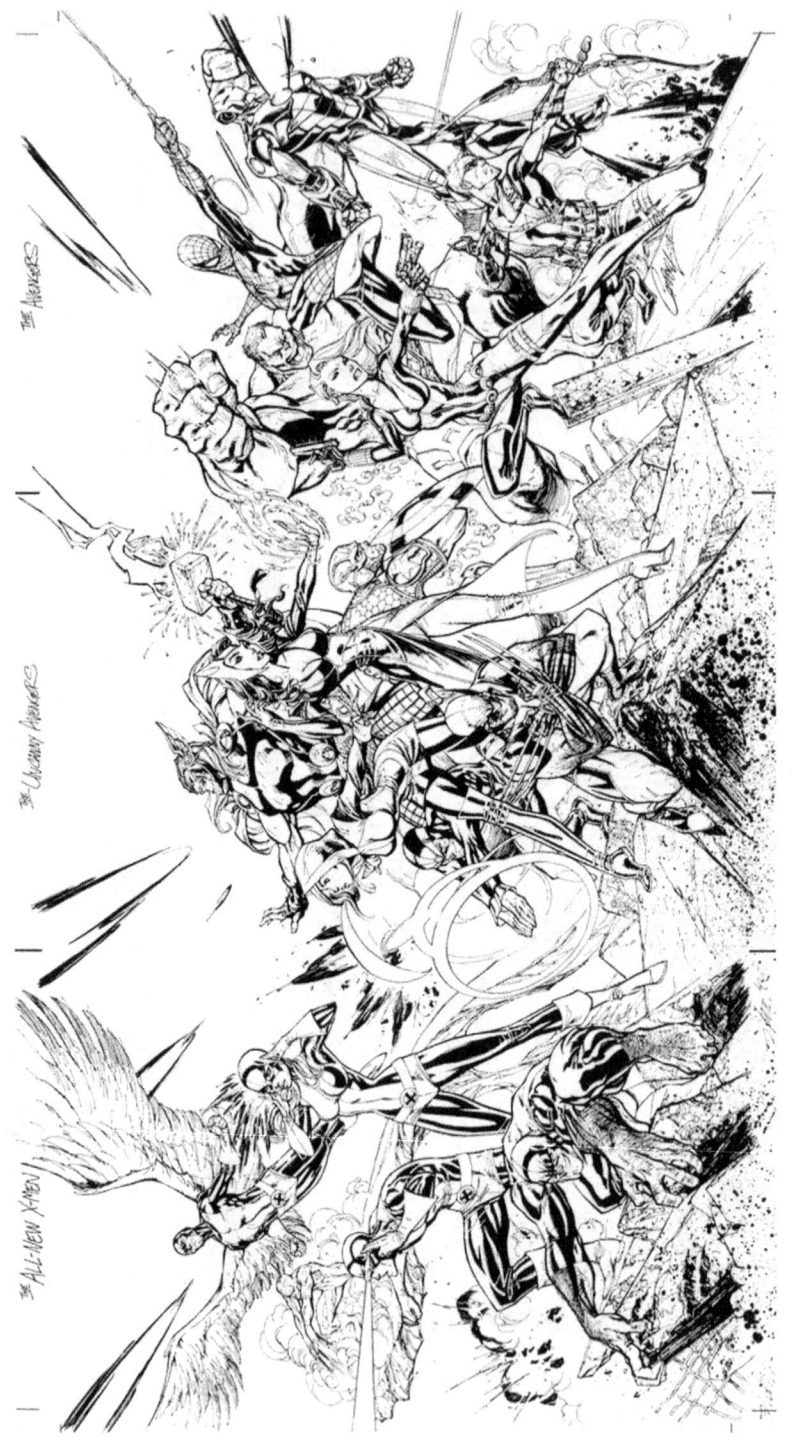

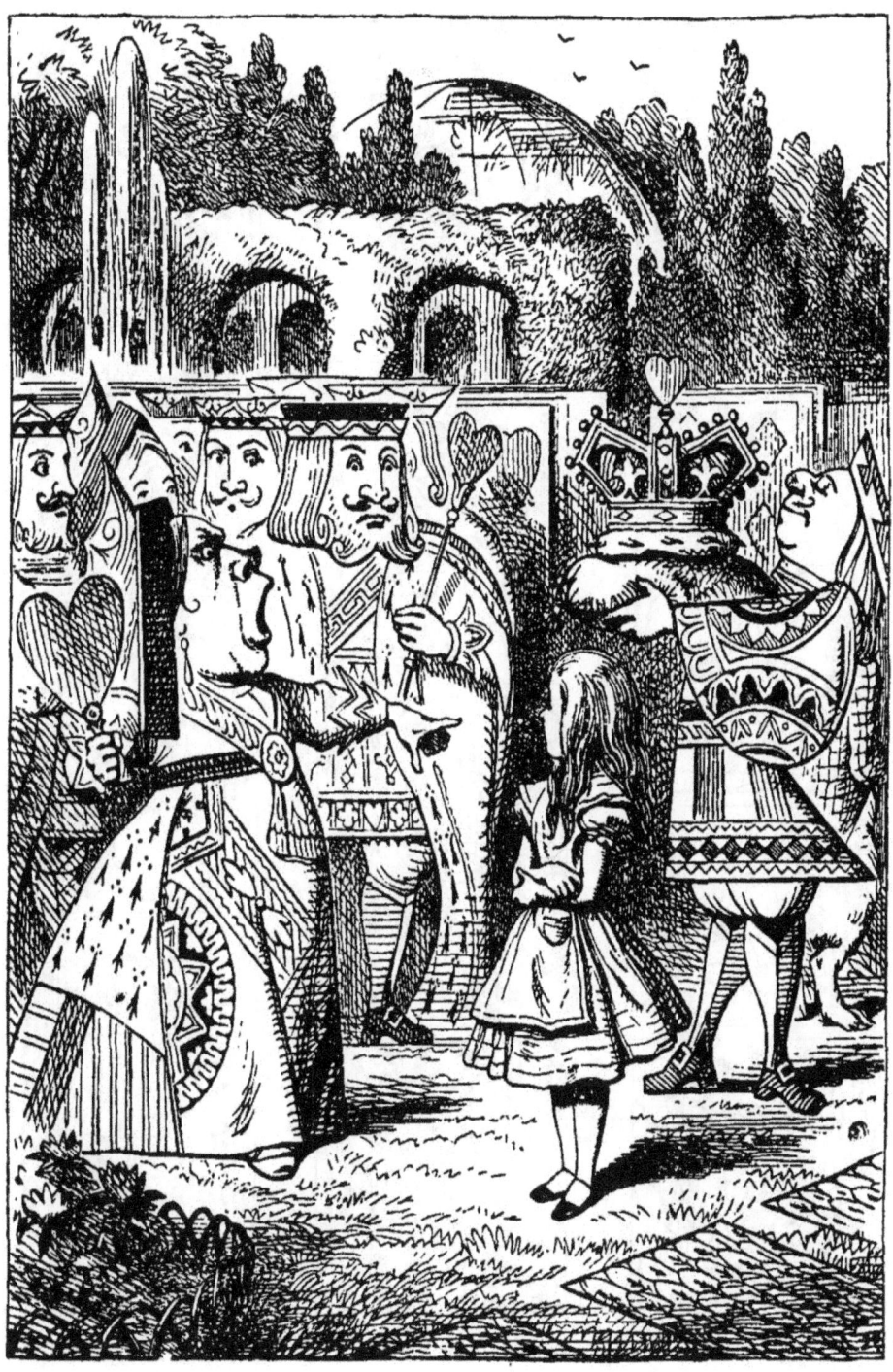

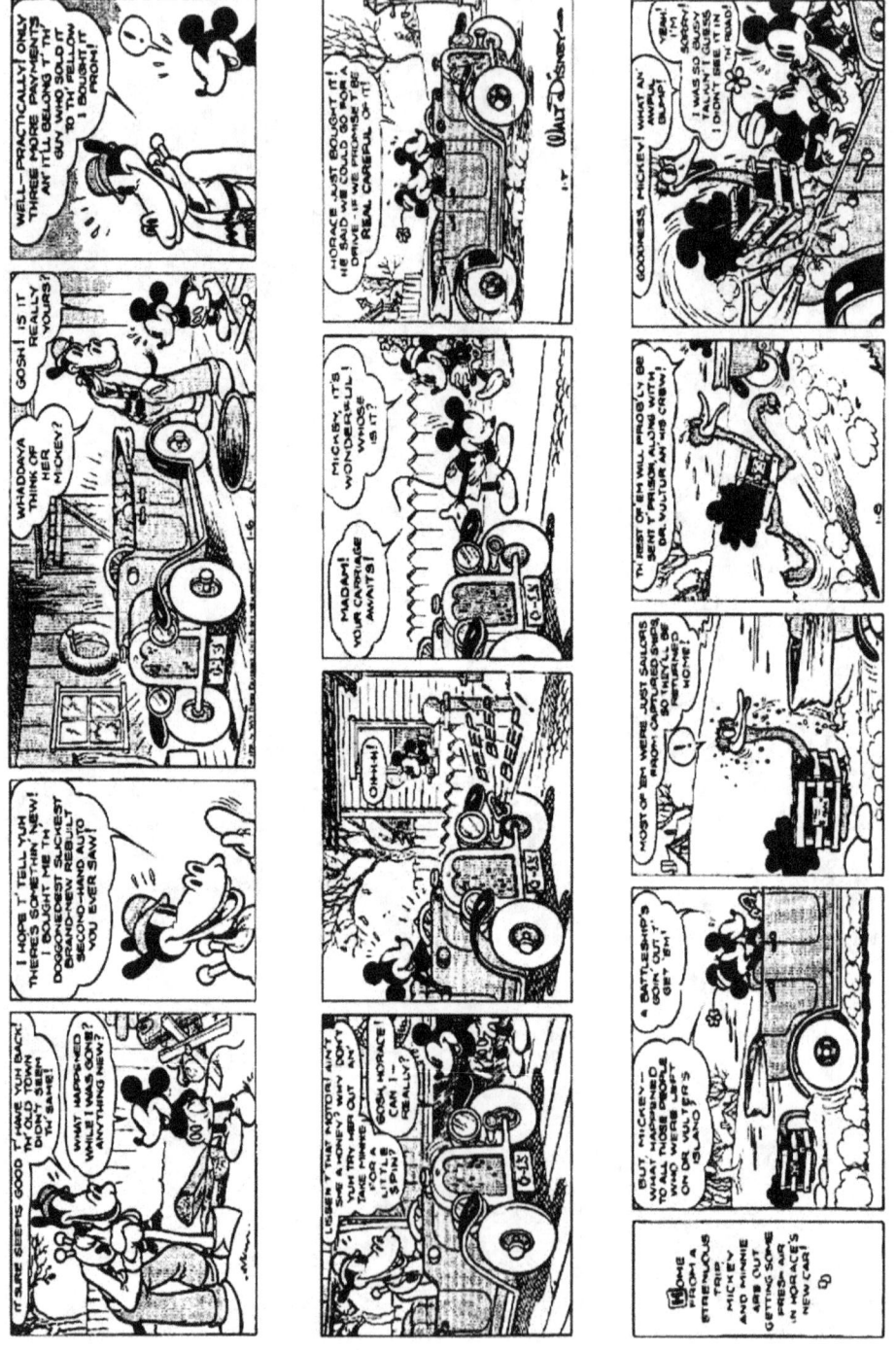

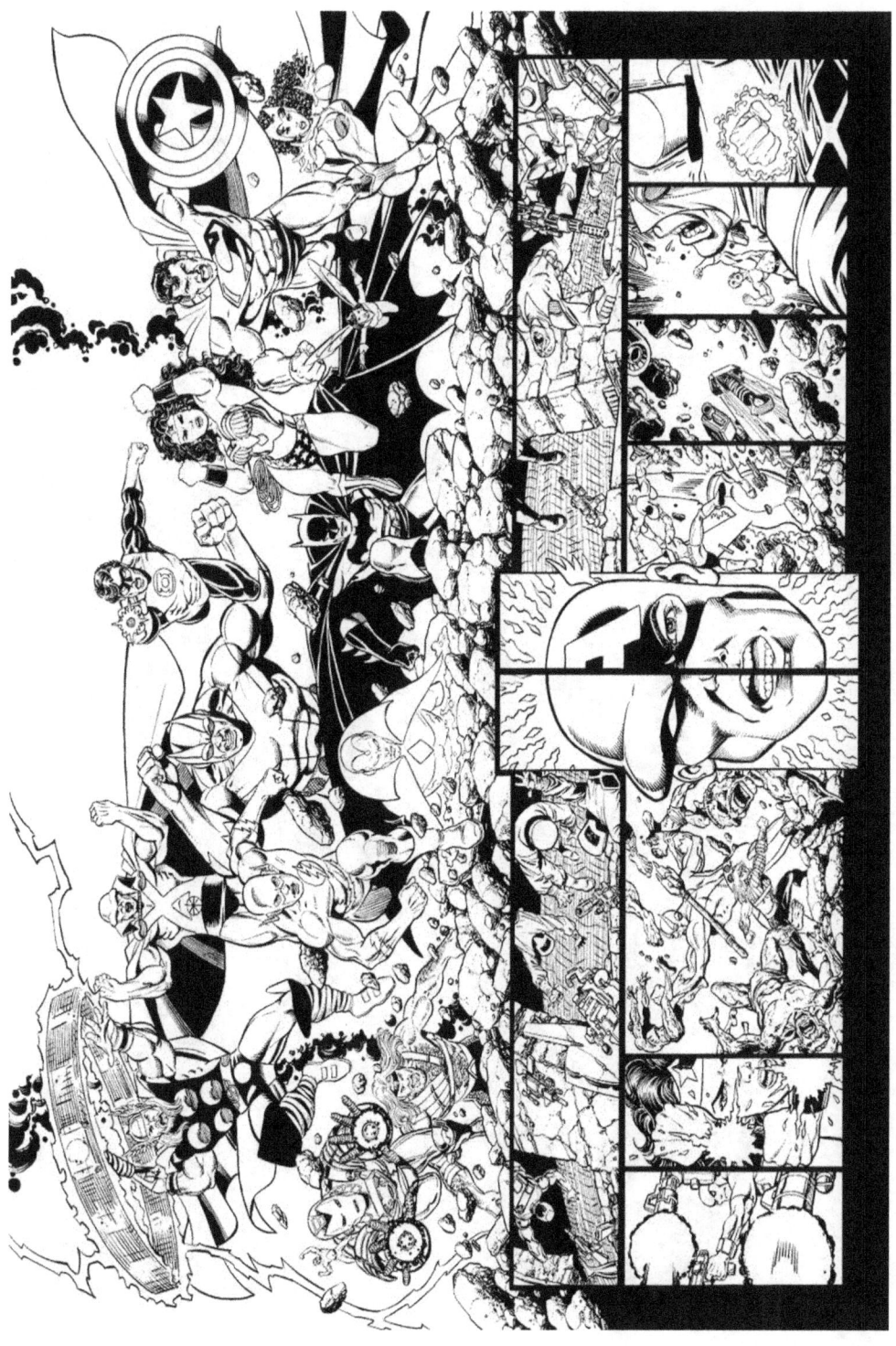

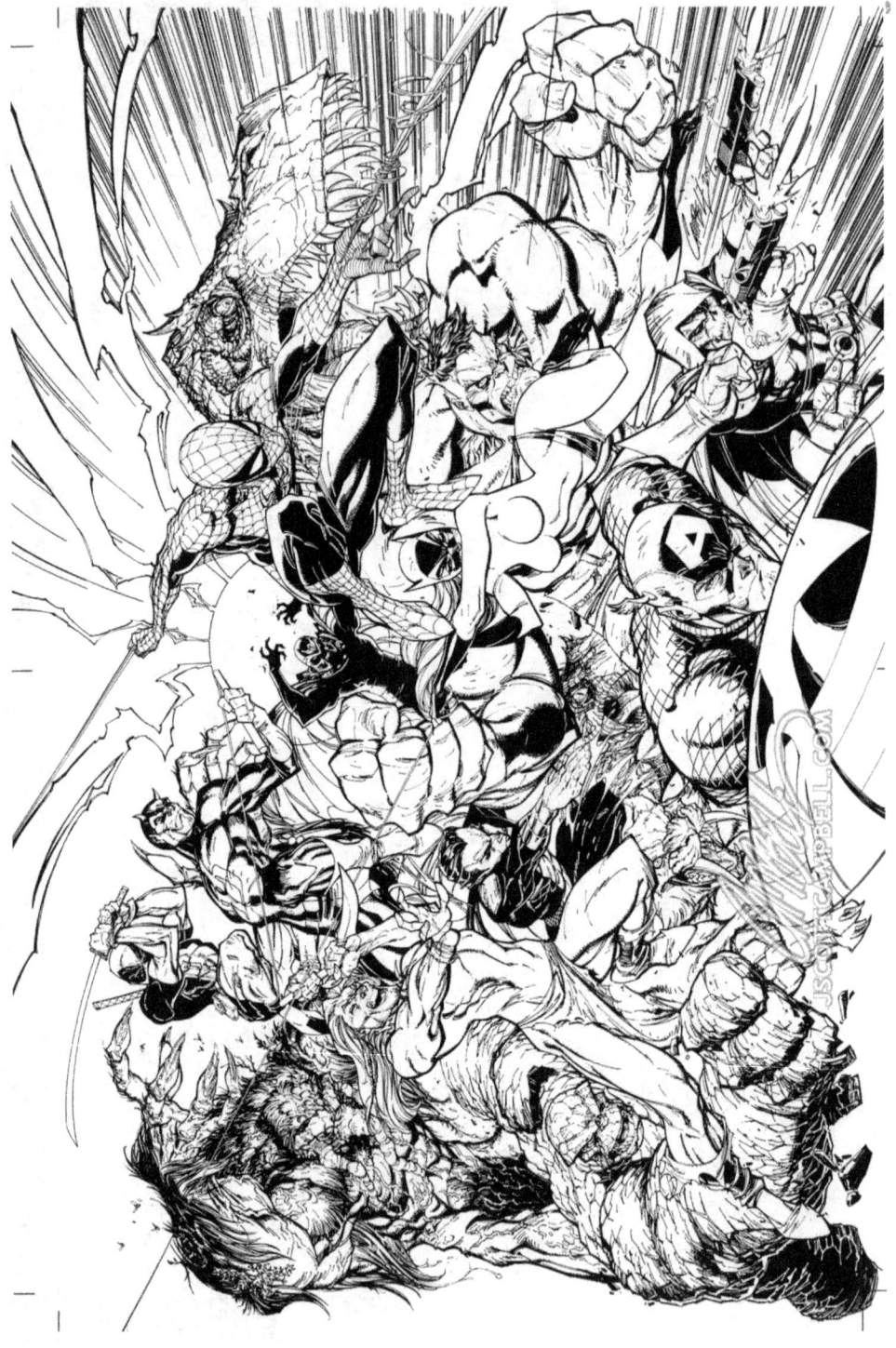

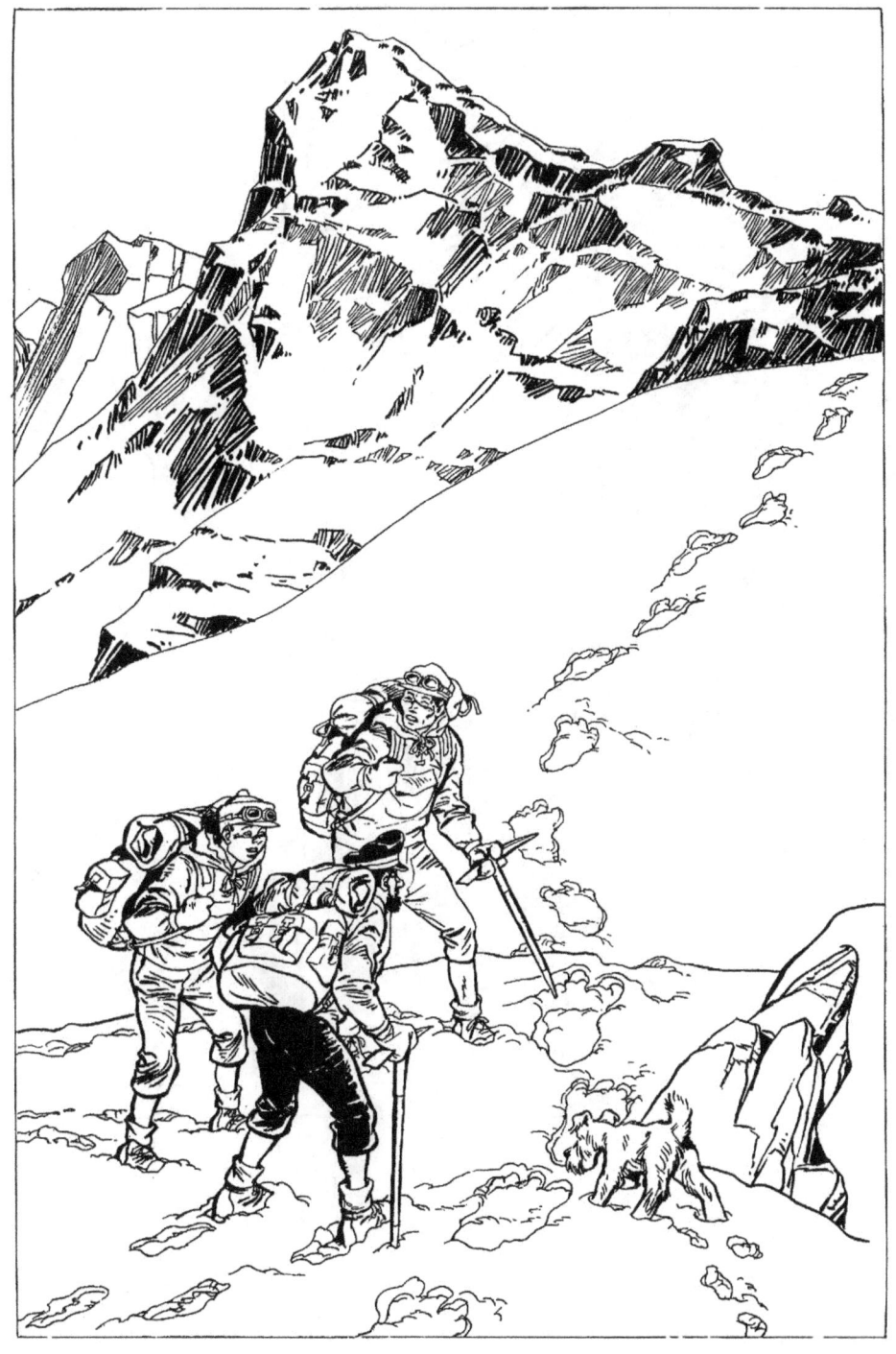

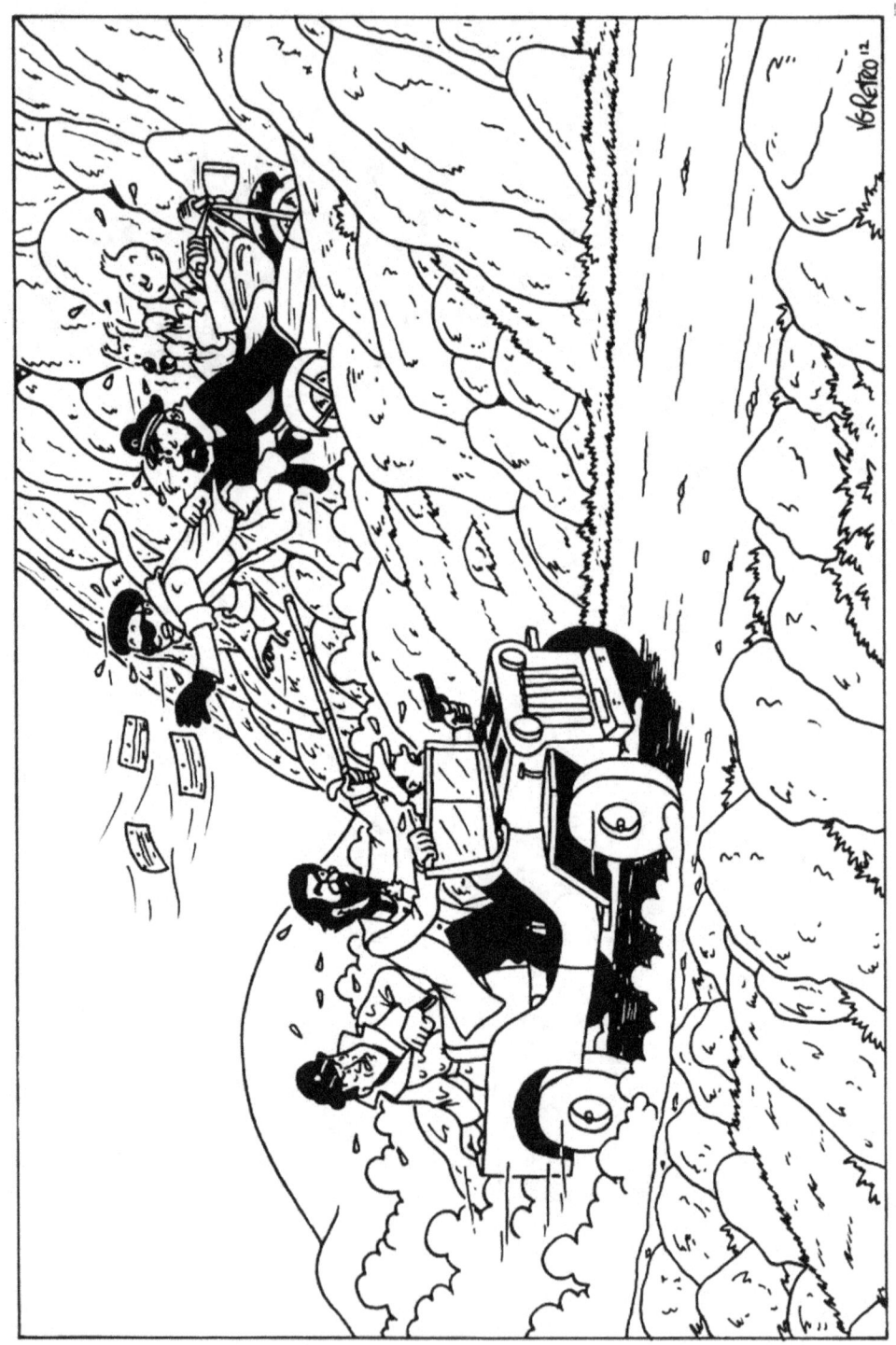

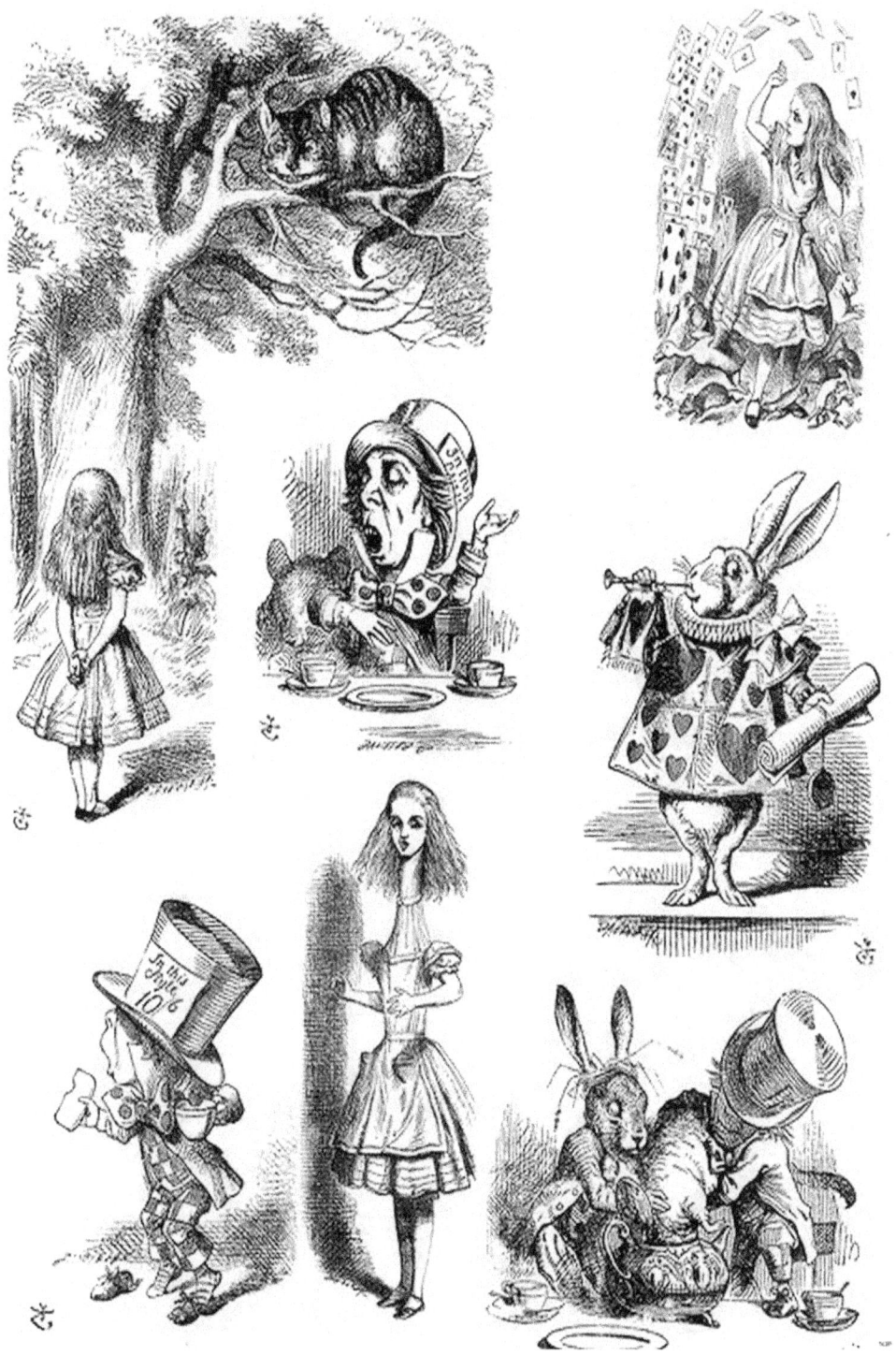

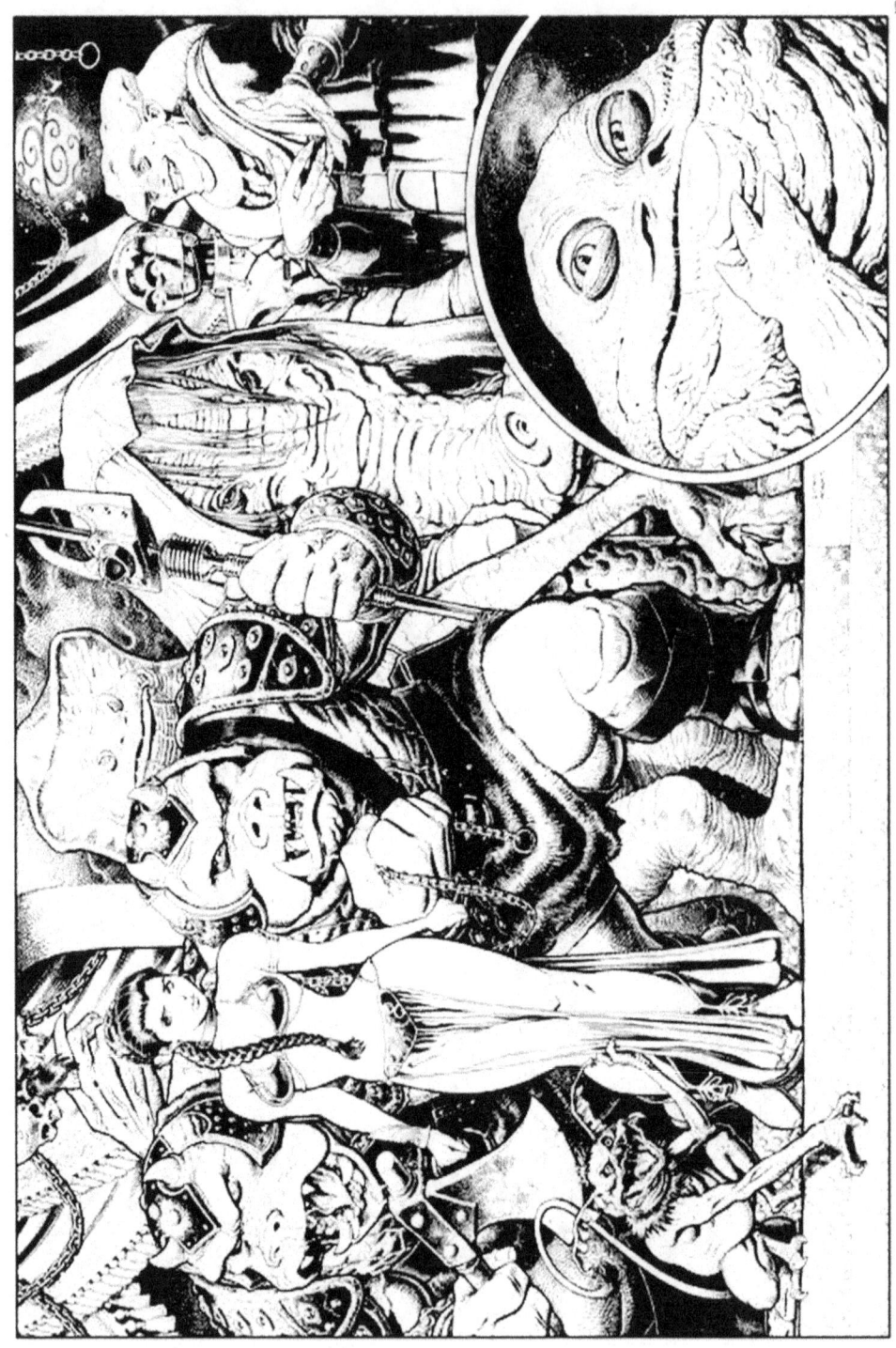

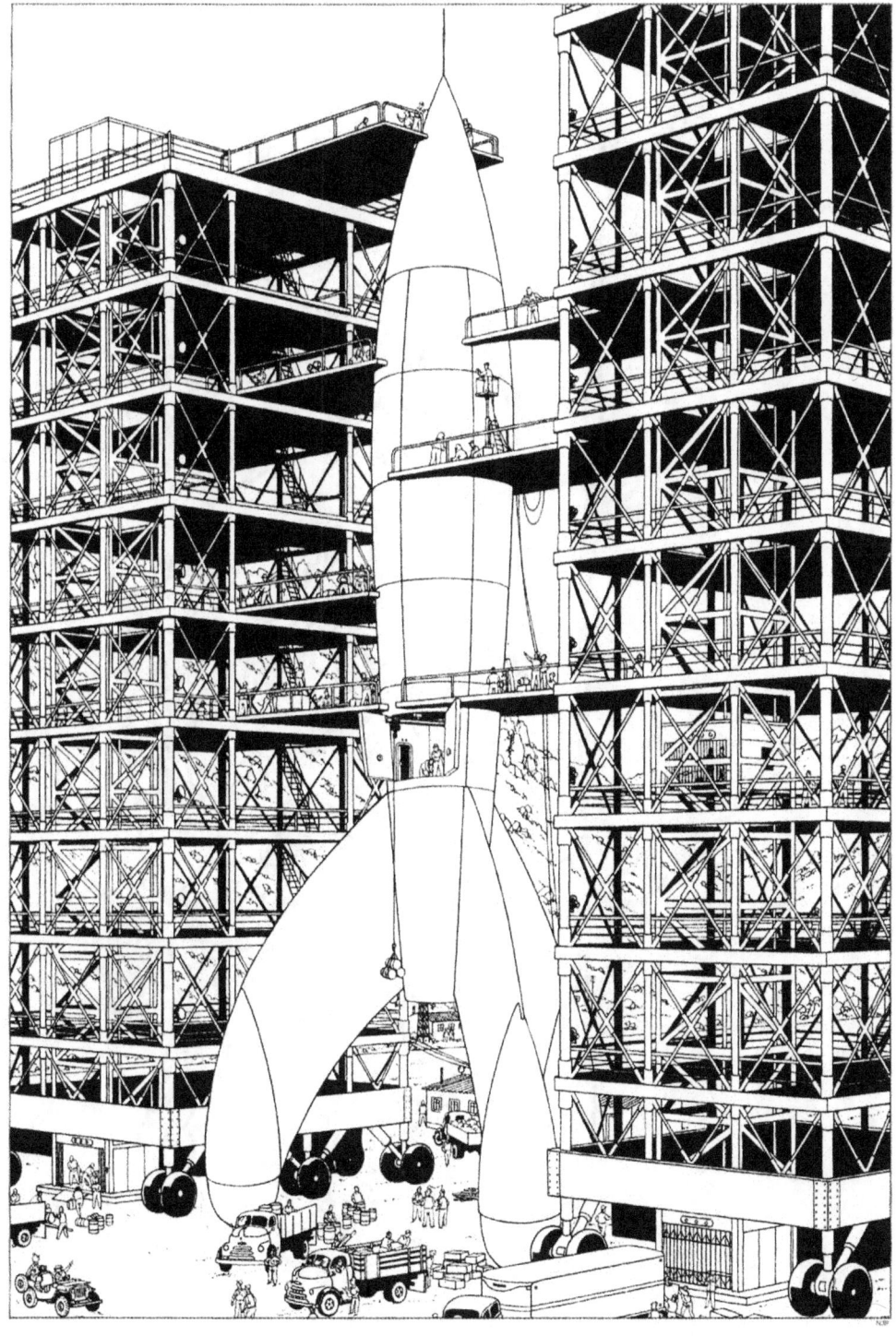

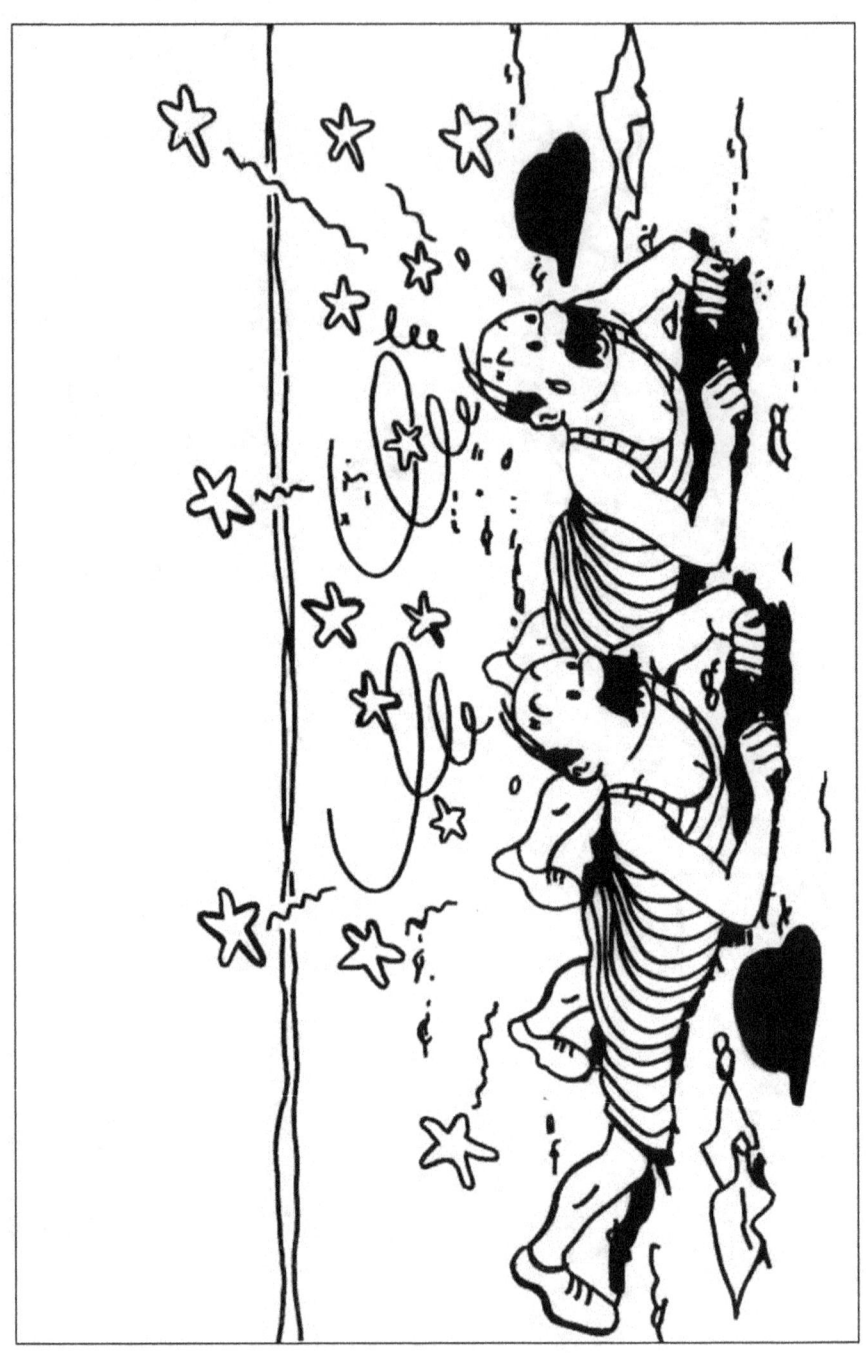

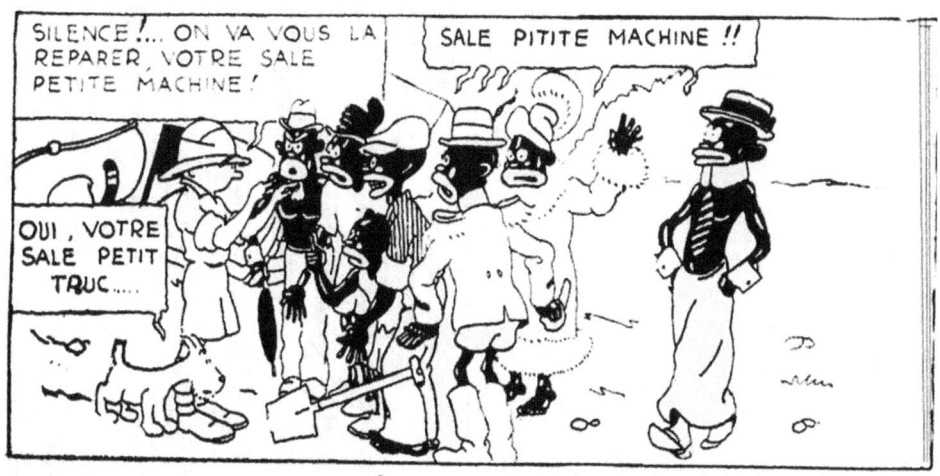

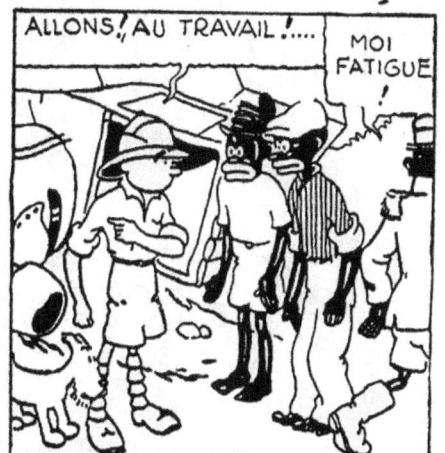

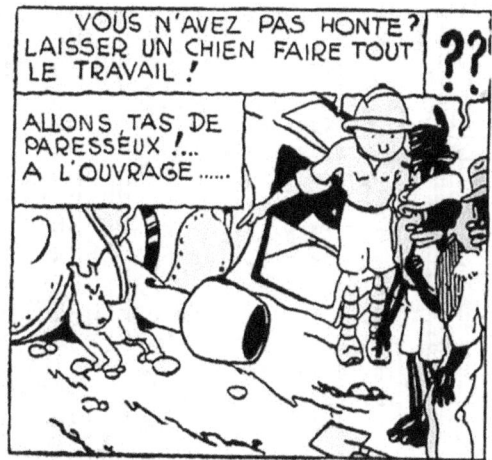

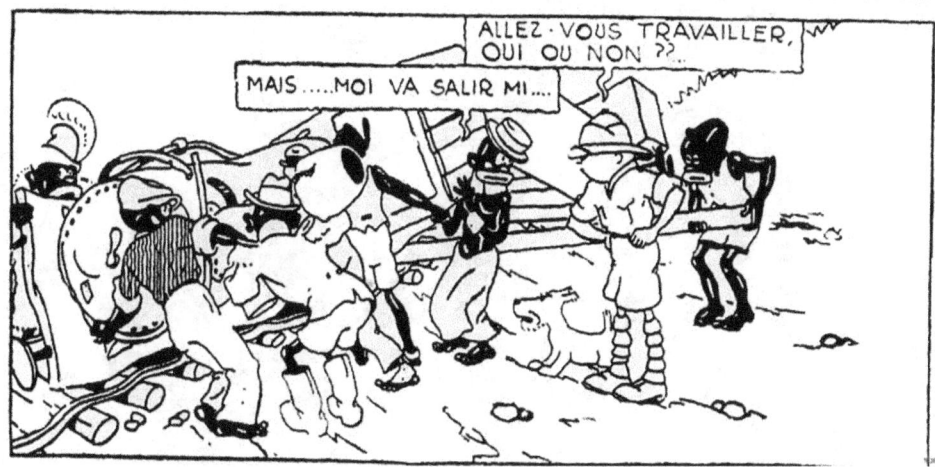

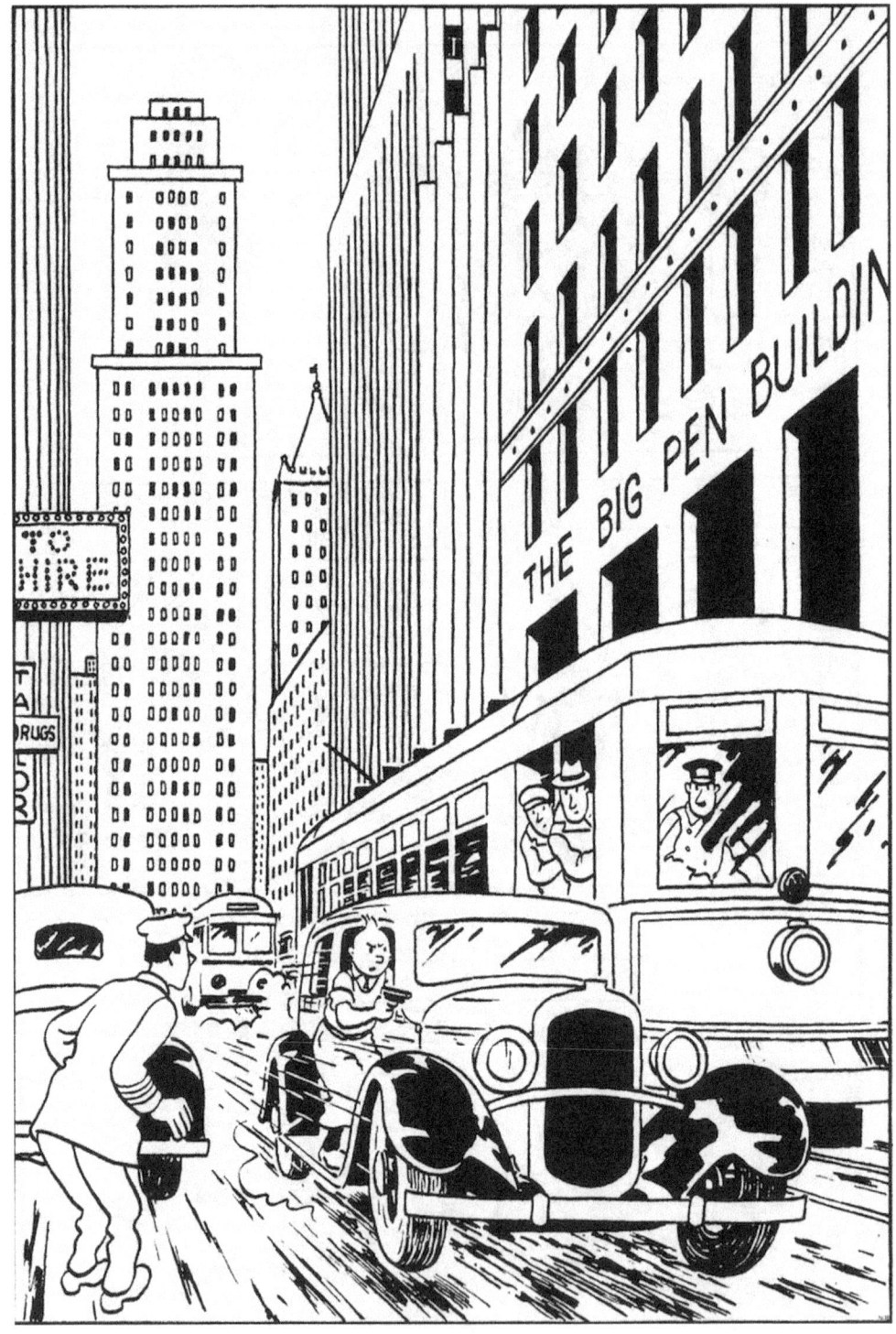

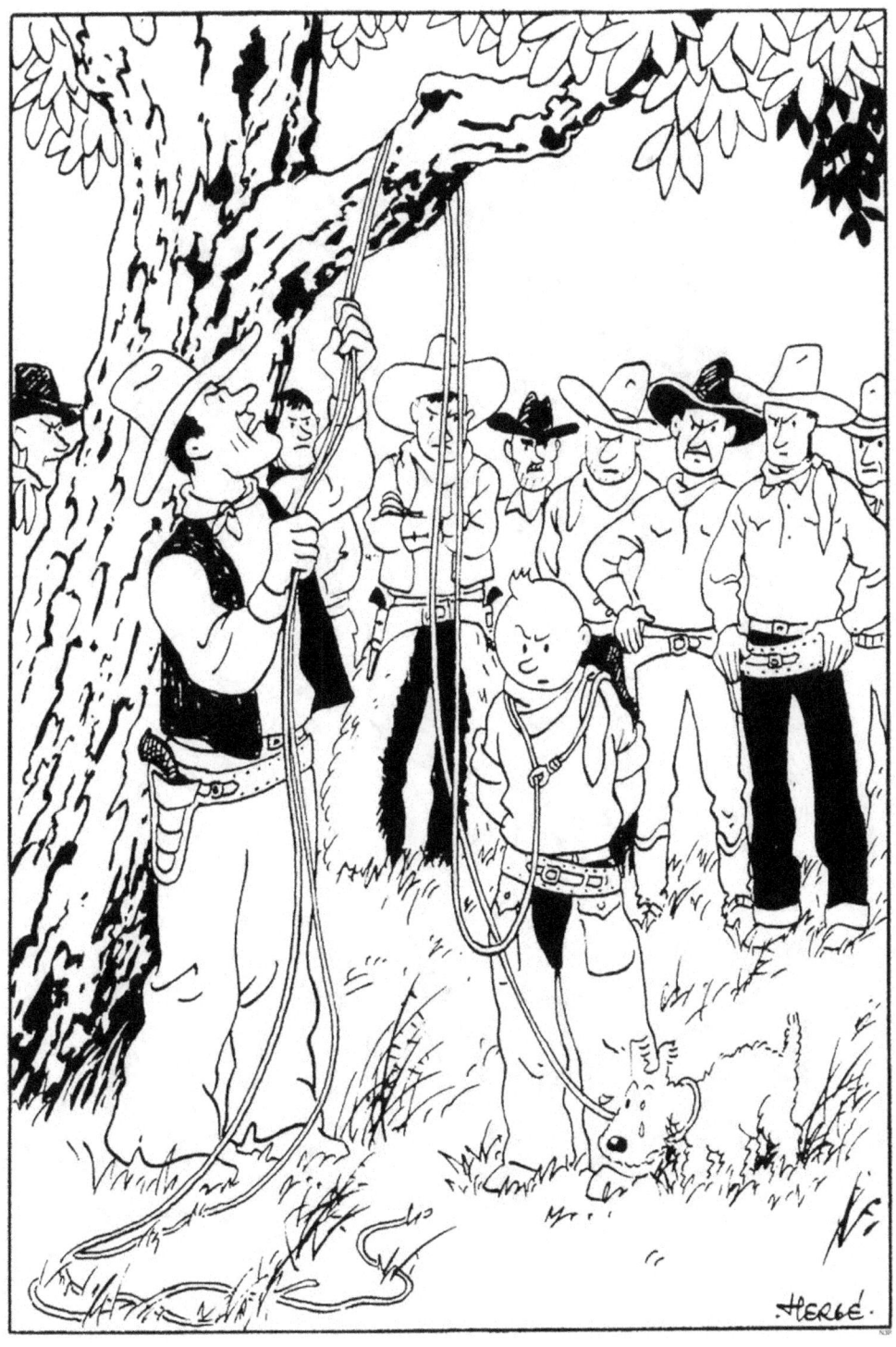

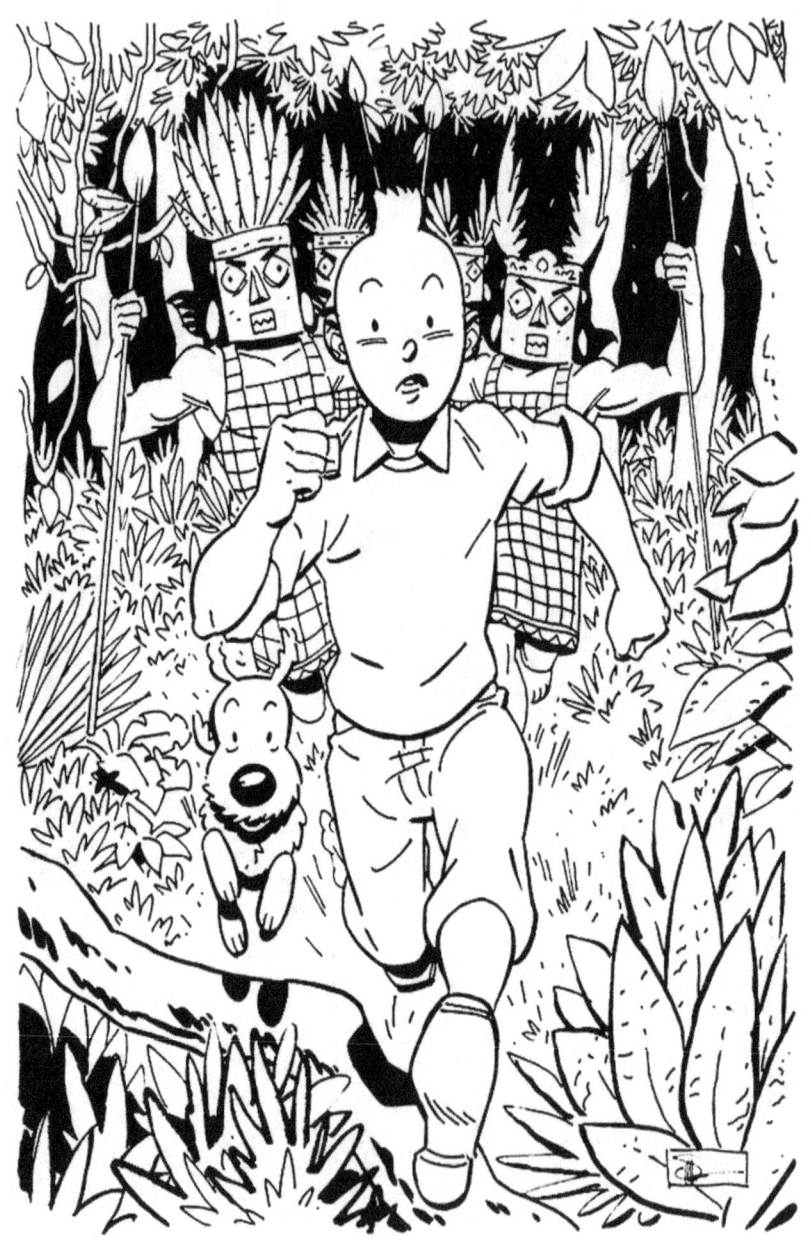

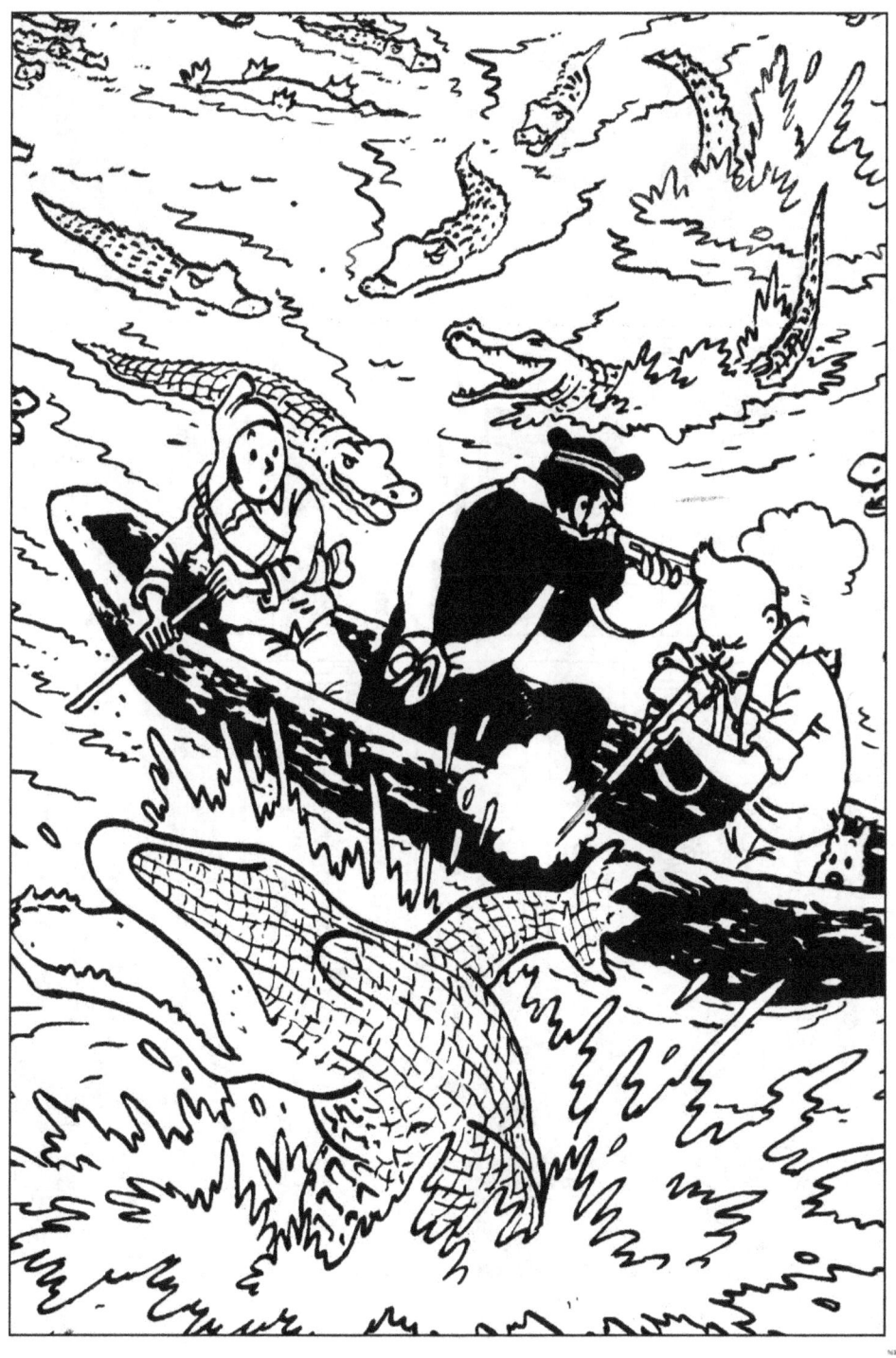

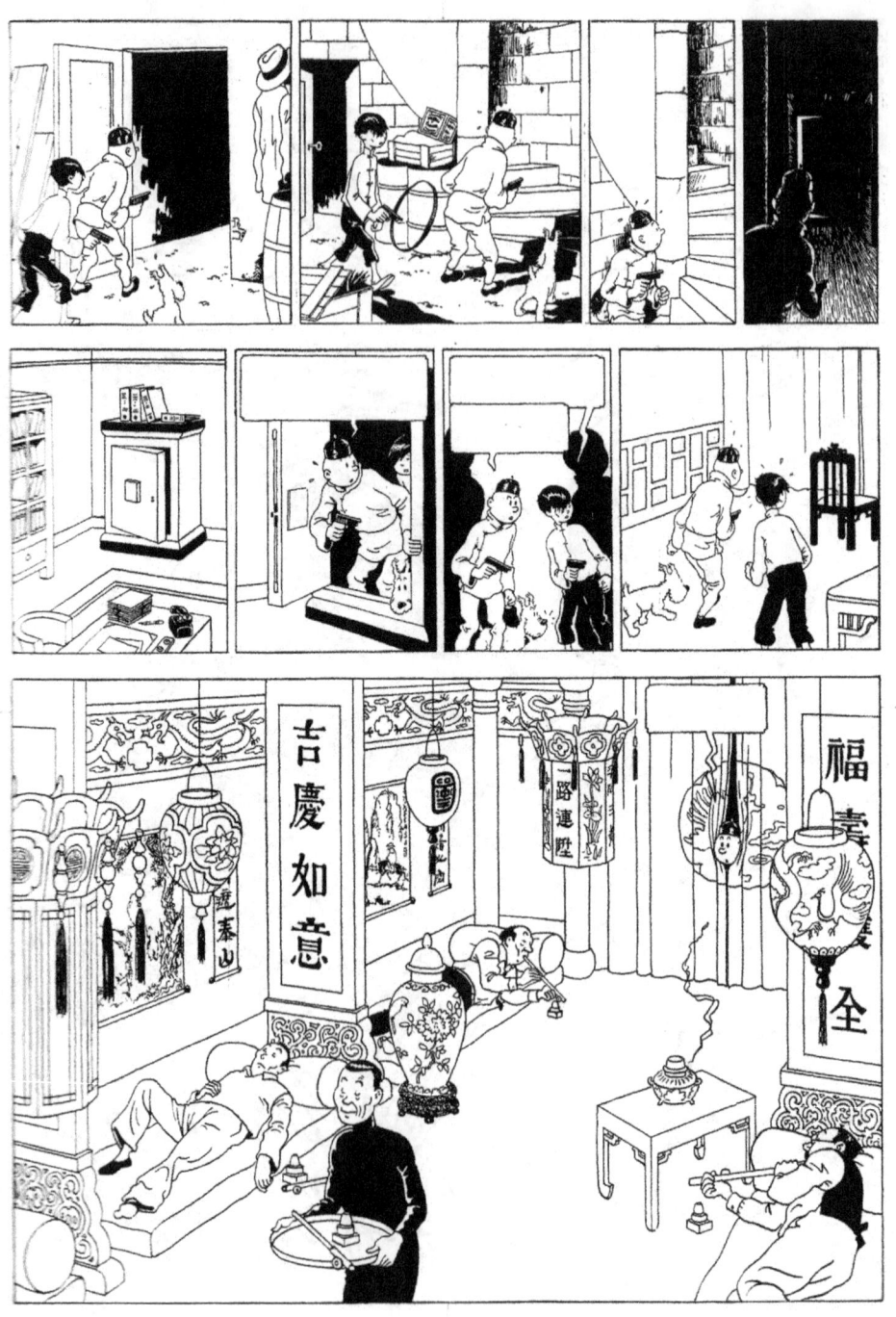

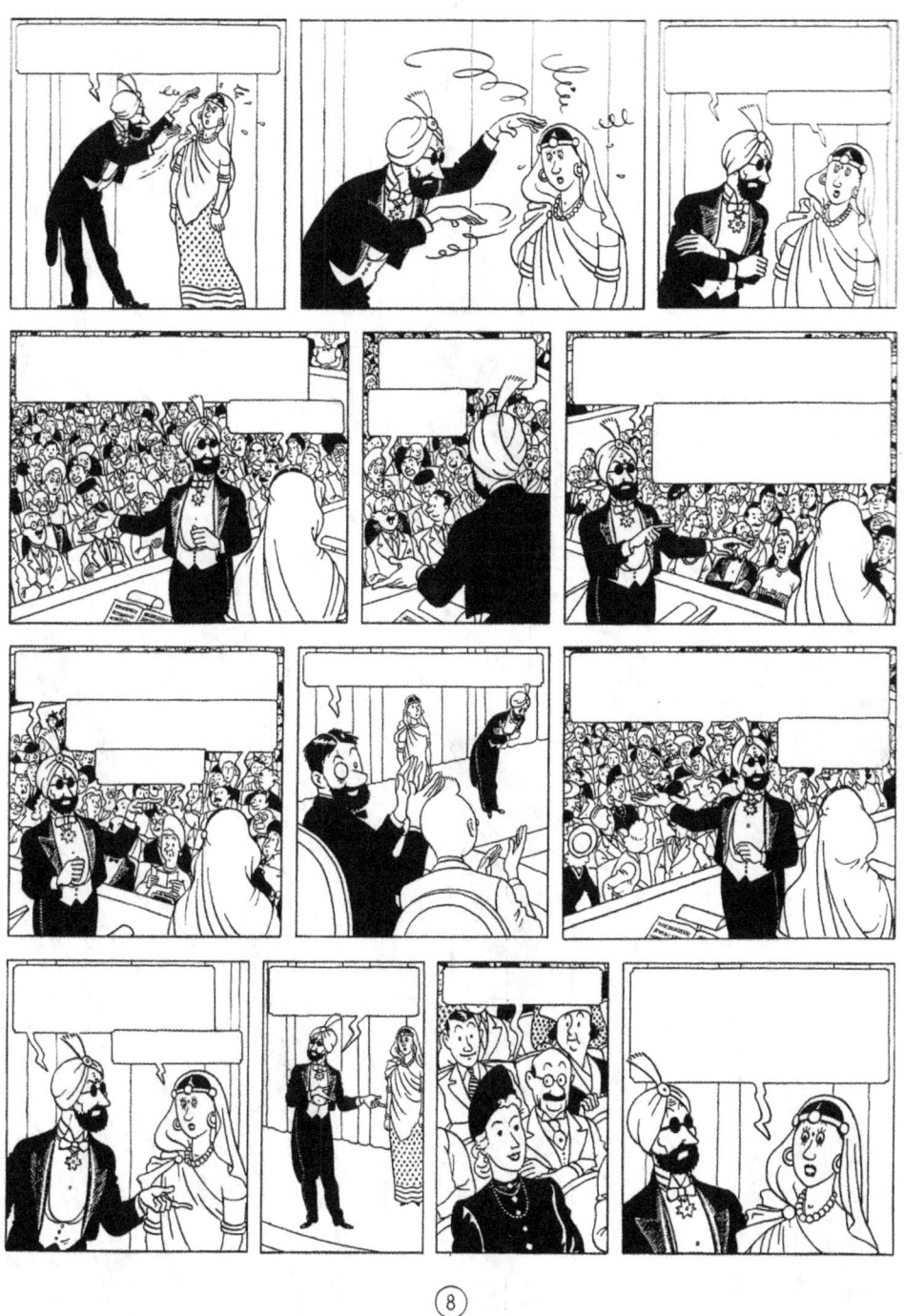

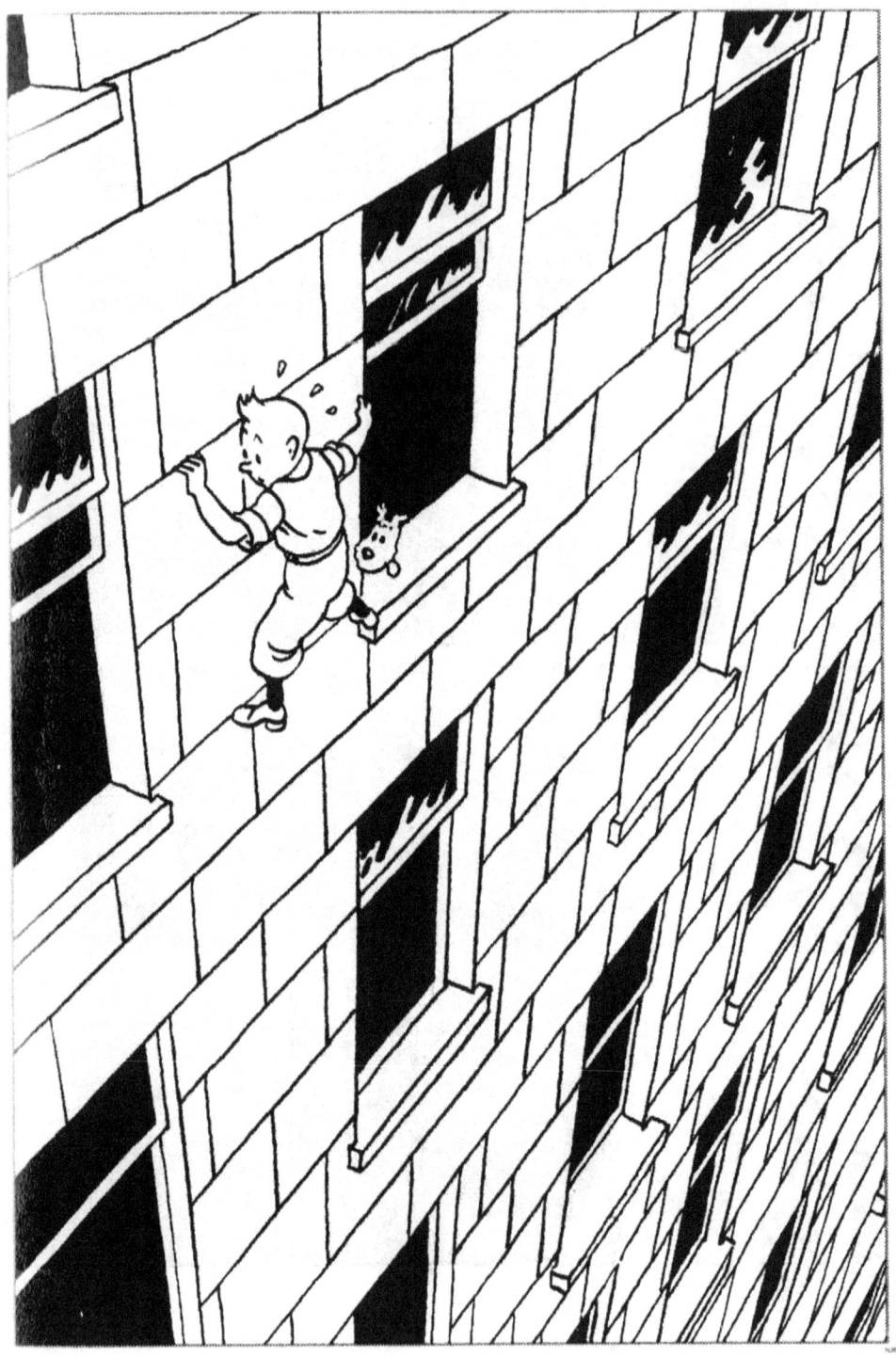

www.ingramcontent.com/pod-product-compliance
Lightning Source LLC
Chambersburg PA
CBHW080559190526
45169CB00007B/2825